The Archangel Book
of
Ritual and Prayer

Ann

may the Angels
bless and keep
you

" MY POWER IS YOUR
POWER, USE IT, LET
IT FLOW, LET IT SHINE ".
AA ZADKIEL.

The Archangelic Book
of
Ritual and Prayer

By

Edwin Courtenay

❧ ❧

Published in the year 2006 by

The Prince of the Stars

The Prince of the Stars
is in the world but not of it.
He is the visionary and builder of a better future.
Therefore he is bringing books telling of love,
healing and a higher consciousness.

© 2006 by Edwin Courtenay
All rights reserved.

Cover Design: Rosi Weiss based on an illustration by
Aeoliah, www.aeoliah.com

Transcriptions: Shirley Flint
Editing and proofreading: Carole Humber
Layout and Typesetting: Hans-Jürgen Maurer

Edition Sternenprinz
P.O. Box 228
79002 Freiburg, Germany

info@sternenprinz.de

ISBN 978-3-929345-27-8
ISBN 3-929345-27-7

DEDICATION

This book is dedicated to my best beloved one and partner Andrew Helme, my soul mate in the truest sense of the word, my hand-fast husband and my own Earth Angel. I thank the Gods and Angels for bringing you into my life.

WITH THANKS

My very special thanks go to Carole Humber for her belief in this book and myself and her tireless efforts in time tabling the work and so diligently checking and correcting the transcript against the tapes. You are truly heaven sent and I do not know what I would do without you in my life.

My thanks also go to my apprentice Kieron Morgan for his friendship and support and for renewing my faith in the faithful and to Shirley Flint for transcribing the channellings.

I would also like to thank my family, Mum and Dad for their constant love and acceptance of my rather unusual lifestyle and for keeping my feet well and truly on the ground. To my sister Jane and her family and my brother Graham and his family for their love and support and to my familiars Rune and Domino for listening to me and loving me when no one else was inclined to!

And finally to the Angels and the Masters and the Goddess and the God for breathing true life into my journey, without you my existence would truly be a grey one.

A NOTE ON RITUAL

Ritual is used to help focus our intent in order to bring about a change in either the world around us or our state of consciousness within. It is not the only way of achieving such changes but for many of us is the required physical link we need to make this happen. If you feel upon reading this book that you would rather enact these rituals on the inner planes, i.e. within the boundaries of your own imagination, or alter the rituals in any way then please feel free to do so. The important thing to remember is that it is the *intent* behind the ritual which provides and shapes the power and therefore this which needs above all other things to be clear and strong.

Contents

List of Rituals and Prayers

ARCHANGEL
❖ METATRON ❖

An Introduction to Angels and Prayer

I am Metatron, the voice of God, higher Archangel of the higher heavens of the celestial and the Divine. I am he who speaks with the word of the Divine Source itself, who gives form and shape to the thoughts and intentions of the Creator. I am the Angel who answers the prayers of mankind and speaks of the instruction of the Divine Plan, of the underlying weave and weft of all creation. I am the beginning as Sandalphon is the end and it has fallen to me to speak with God's words in the beginning of this, this tome of wisdom, this guide, offered and extended in love and trust and grace and peace and truth by the guardians of light, the Angels of the higher heavens. It has fallen to me to extend guidance that seeks to be offered by the Divine in order that man may more clearly understand the nature of the angelic kingdom, their source and origin and function and the reason for their interaction with mankind.

In the beginning, long before time and space existed, when there was only the Divine Source, a perfect blend of masculine and feminine energy, of positive and negative polarities, there were no Angels, we did not exist. The Divine was growing in consciousness, becoming more and more aware of itself as being everything, expanding in awareness to fill the vastness of its omni-directional being, its own multidimensional nature. It was only when the Divine Source became completely aware of its infinite nature that it decided that it would create a limited space and time in order to further explore its own nature in circumstances and situations that were at that moment in time beyond its ken; limitation and condition. In order to bring about the manifestation of this unknown quantity the Divine decided to create extensions of its own being that would aid in the creation of this complex plan, aspects of its own unique consciousness to fulfil its desires and wishes so that its own attention could be focused on other more pressing situations that required its full attention and focus. And so the Divine began to splinter itself into other subsequent beings, to create aspects of its own perfect radiance, born from its central core, from its love and intense curiosity, from its need to grow, from its thirst and hunger for knowledge and evolution, for enlightenment and understanding. And so in limitless space and in no time the first Angels were created. The first Angels that were created were collective forces, groups of Angels who were symbiotically bonded together and worked as a whole. They were created initially to monitor over the infinite radiance of the Divine, to help the Divine remain contained, focused, to help the Divine remain controlled so that the manifestation could be brought about smoothly and with the minimum of exertion of energy, flowing in accordance with an economy of energy which would enable and ensure that nothing would be wasted, that everything would occur efficiently and in accordance with perfect timing and perfect grace.

It was only when the Divine created limited space and time with the aid of those Angels, the architects of the universe known as "the Demiurge" that the Divine placed itself into limited space, into temporal space for the first time. The division that occurred was unexpected. The Divine's energy became segmented in accordance to frequency division and the Divine's radiance became dissolved, as white light becomes dissolved through a prism into the aspects of its beautiful spectrum. The Divine became divided into masculine and feminine, positive and negative, but also its consciousness became divided into a mental and emotional status as well as falling into some of the denser vibrational expressions of reality, into matter and form. Angels in limited space and time were created from a frequency of the Divine's consciousness known as "the heart of the Divine Source", other beings being created from an aspect of the consciousness called "the mind of the Divine Source", mankind and the mineral kingdom, for instance, were created from this segment of the Divine's expression. But before elementals and human nature were created, Angels were formed from the heart of the Divine Source to monitor over the further creation and manifestation of matter in the physical universe, in the lower dimensions and realities. Initially collectives were formed here, the Cherubim and the Seraphim for instance, who would monitor over the powerful energies of love within the universe and the fabric of space time reality. But in time other Angels were created also, Angels of a singular nature who would oversee and govern specific elements and energies, who would have specific duties and tasks to perform.

The first singular Angel to be created was Lucifer but Lucifer himself will speak of his creation and his duties and his tasks a little later on in this book. The other Angels to be born were Sandalphon and Michael, Ratziel and Raphael, Melchizadek and Gabriel, Azrael and so on. Melchizadek is a particular and specific angelic frequency becoming at this moment in time more known to mankind for his unique properties, who exists on the cusp between non-reality and reality as you know it. But once again he himself will speak of his own unique nature and although Lucifer is considered to be the first Angel to be born because he was the first singular angelic force to be manifest within limited space and time, Melchizadek is in essence the first Angel who dabbled his toes within reality, being born on the outer edge of nonreality and bridging the divide between these two unique spaces and dimensions. And so in time the angelic continuum was created. My kind were born and knew existence inside and outside of limited space and time and we began to fulfil our function in accordance with the Divine's will.

Now it is important to remember that Angels were created as extensions of the Divine's consciousness and therefore in essence we have no free-will consciousness of our own. We are the Divine and the Divine is us. We have no need for a free will because our will is the will of the Divine. Providing us with free will would be unnecessary unless we were created in order to have a form of improvisational skill which is reserved for only one band of Angels who were indeed given a degree of this power: the Demiurge, the architects of the universe. All other angelic forms then have no free will of their own but operate purely from the will of the Divine Source. We are a collective consciousness and although we have individual existence, purpose and properties, we are bound together through our commonality, connected and attuned, aligned and at one. We live in a continuum, a stream of existence in which there is in essence no hierarchical system but simply a manifestation of frequency ranging from high to low.

Visualise then our continuum if you will as a three-sided pyramid. At the base of the pyramid there are the lower angelic frequencies and forms; the Guardian Angels and those beneath them who preside over the everyday, run of the mill, mundane existences of reality. And then at the peak of the pyramid there are the higher Angels of the higher heavenly host from celestial divisions; the collectives and the archangelic forms who preside over more cosmic elements and importances. It is apparent by looking at the pyramid that there is a higher pinnacle and that there is a lower foundation and yet it is also apparent that this form is one, it is a whole, a solid object. Therefore, this is how the continuum is; there is no point of breakage, there is no line that marks the top and the bottom, there simply is a higher and lower point and yet the form, the shape, is all one. This is how our consciousness is; co-joined, connected, all one and yet exhibiting higher and lower expressions of Divine existence and vibration.

The angelic continuum then was created in order to manifest limited space and time and then to govern over the elemental energies and forces that reign within it. To protect its integrity, to guard over its fabric, to ensure that nothing harms or hinders its progression and expansion, its existence, to maintain the flow of the Divine Plan and purpose within it; God's desire to understand itself within limited space and time through the manifestation of mankind and reality, through the expression of Divine consciousness, through matter, whether that is animal, mineral, vegetable, mankind or planetary in nature and also the unseen, unformed entities and life forms that know expression in other dimensions which interpenetrate your own. We were also created in order to guide life forms within the universe, to offer assistance and help, direction, rescue, understanding. To help encourage the life forms that exist within your universe to journey back to their source, to return to the Divine through the process of evolution and ascension.

This is our connection to you. We were created to be your guides, to be your helpers, to be your inspirations, to be your muse. We were created to be your protectors and guardians, to remind you of the presence of the Divine in reality and this is what we have always done since the beginning of your time. We have known many shapes and many forms and as most learned people are aware are not presences or beings which are particularly connected to any one religion that exists upon your planet, or any other planet for that matter. Although most people associate the word "Angel" with Christianity, we have known many different names and shapes and forms throughout history and time and often we are spoken of by these names and addressed through these archetypes without mankind ever understanding or believing that we are in fact one and the same. We are the Divine Source, God, expressions of this one true light. We are the presence of the Divine given shape and form and understanding through mankind's comprehension but beyond that on a larger scale we are elemental, essential, integral expressions of the division of the Divine's might and power.

Within us, created by the Divine Source, is an immeasurable love. It is a love for those that we have been created to serve and aid. It is a desire to cosset and nurture, to care and protect, to guide and strengthen and aid. We are limited in the way in which we can fulfil our expression because of the Divine Plan itself and the nature of the higher self's will. The Divine Source and we do not possess the power to circumvent the will of the higher self. It is a gift given to souls by the Divine Source at the beginning of time, the power of free will. This free will means that souls can choose not to follow the path that is laid before them by the Divine, not to adhere to the Divine Plan or blueprint, not to obey God's suggestion or command but simply to do as they will.

We love mankind and all life forms that exist within your

universe and strive in accordance with the parameters that are set to us to aid mankind in all and any way that we can but our consciousness is different from your own and as such we do not see sometimes those things that you believe to be assistance that we should offer and give. We are eternal and infinite, we have always been. Before we were given form and structure we were elements of consciousness within the Divine. We have existed then before our angelic status as thoughts and understandings. Now we are given form we understand more about the nature of existence but the majority of us have not existed and although some of us have crossed the streams and incarnated into physical form and flesh, we still have little to no comprehension of the nature of limitation and physical existence. Pain, age, tragedy; these things are concepts which are abstract to us. We see and feel what takes place within mankind as they age and die, as they become ill and experience horror and pain but we can find no point of comparison within our own being. Even when we are incarnate in physical form there is a part of our divinity that is always aware that what we experience is simply illusion. We offer then what we can but we cannot concern ourselves with those things that we know to be unreal or untrue. We steer mankind towards their greatest spiritual expression and if that path and course dictates that they must suffer then we will endeavour to do all that we can to aid them in processing and understanding the need for this suffering but we will not guide them away from it if it is what they need to experience in order to grow.

Angels then can be seen as all-compassionate, loving and giving, great sources of harmony and light, which we are, but we can also be seen as harsh and cold and cruel, as unemotional, uncaring, faceless blocks of ice who would simply point mankind towards one goal without any care for the pain and suffering that it will cause, and in its own emotive way this also is true. We must flow in accordance with God's will; God desires evolution for mankind and evolution can only be reached by experiencing the negative as well as the positive.

I am Metatron, the voice of God. I speak God's words on Earth and to the heavenly hosts, the angelic continuum, for God the Divine Source is an infinite being and its words in their purity cannot be heard on Earth or even felt within the angelic continuum that exists within limited space and time without causing destruction. The Divine Force in the unlimited universe, in the universe that has no time, that exists beyond it, is wild like a raging sun, maintained and held in check by elements of its own consciousness, collective angelic forces that were created in order to ensure its integrity, function, focus and purpose. I am a filter. I am a representation. I am a transformer and translator. I speak the words of the Divine safely in the realms of limitation so that they may be heard, and as such in part am also responsible for answering the prayers of mankind. Sandalphon, my twin, who resides in the lowest sphere as bastion and overseer of the physical earthly plane, is responsible for gathering the prayers of mankind together and sending them to the Divine. The Divine then passes on these answers to me and I distribute them back towards the physical plane.

Prayer is a powerful thing, underestimated and unrecognised by most, abandoned, unfortunately, by many. It is not simply an invocation that brings forward miraculous manifestation in accordance with the querant's requests but an opportunity to enter into powerful communication with the Creator force, opening oneself as a conduit and vessel through which the light of the Divine may pour, providing not only guidance but also a connection of profound and deep unity and love. Prayers are answered not only in the literal way. The era of the burning, talking bush has passed and now God speaks through omens and portents, through dreams and visions granted in meditations and in daydreams, through the words of others, through slogans that our eye accidentally roves upon, through impressions that we receive, intuitions, inner knowings, through our conscience and our sub-conscious mind. These are the ways in which the Divine answers your prayers through me and these are the things that you must look to see in order to know the truth of the Great Spirit. And so in bringing this, the first discourse, to an end we would speak of prayer.

It does not matter to whom you verbally address your prayer. Prayer is an act of intent. The intent is to establish a connection with the Divine Source, to surrender ourselves to this presence, to surrender our worries and our concerns, our requests and our desires and also, hopefully, to offer to the Divine Presence some form of devotion. Devotion is a very misunderstood word. People of certain faiths and reli-gions believe that the Divine requires of mankind worship; the Divine does not. It does not require worship in order to exist or maintain its existence. Worship is required only if the individual who worships desires to anchor and ground and feel the presence of the Divine in their life and their environment. Devotional practice, whether it is the offering of praise or gratitude or thanks, the burning of incense or of candlelight, the offering of flowers or fruits upon a table, is the process whereby the divine radiance of the Source is grounded, anchored through the sacrifice. The sacrifice is one in which intention, desire and sometimes a representa-tion of life force energy is burnt or offered in order for the absence of it to create a space which the light of the Divine may fill. The light of the candle burns so that the light of the Divine may take its place on Earth. Incense is dissolved into the air so that the absence of that that once was is filled with the presence of the Divine's truth. Fruit and flowers wither and die upon an altar and are offered to the ground so that the absence of their life force presence may be filled with the presence of God. Songs and praises, worship, gratitude and prayer are offered so that these words spoken, these thoughts expressed, this energy spent, may be replaced by the presence of the Infinite Source.

Devotion as part of prayer then guarantees the presence of the Divine, creates a space in which the Divine may enter and anchor itself around the querant so that their prayers may indeed be answered. The surrendering of our prayers totally and completely, the knowledge that the Divine knows our thoughts and our feelings and therefore that we have in essence no need to vocalise or specifically speak them, enables us to more totally enter into a state of communion with the Higher Presence. When we open ourselves to God, when we surrender ourselves to the Divine Source in this way, when we offer our devotion, we enter into a state of unity. This unity is very important, for often that which we seek can only be answered through the feeding of our spirit. It is not guidance that we need, it is not miraculous manifestation. It is connection with the Source. When we are connected with the Source we are filled with an awareness of hope and faith and trust. We are granted the gift of grace and flow, synchronicities bloom into our life, we are given strength and healing and we are shown what to do. Not always and necessarily by the Divine Source itself but sometimes by the clearer connection that is made between our lower consciousness and our higher consciousness, between the lower self and the higher self, the soul, or because our spiritual faculties here on Earth are opened so that we may more clearly see the road that has always lain ahead of us.

Entering into a state of unity and community with the Divine through prayer is a powerful way of staying connected to our true origin and essence, remaining integral in our focus and alignment to our higher source and in connection with the synchronicities of our spiritual journey and path. Too many people clasp their hands together, babble off a shopping list of requests and then depart, lighting a candle, burning some incense, offering a hymn with no conscious knowledge of what they do or why. The presence of the Divine begins to warm the space around them but before it can step forwards and begin to offer the information that the individual seeks, the individual is gone. Prayer is an act of dynamism and receptivity. The dynamic act is offering our devotion and our confusion, our desires, our request, our fears. The act of reception is waiting for the Divine Presence to enter into the space that we have created through this act and provide us with that that we require. What follows is mindfulness. Being aware of our thoughts or the people, places or situations that we might enter into whereby our prayer might be answered. Not always through miraculous manifestation but sometimes simply through guidance given.

In prayer then acknowledge what you do. The space around you becomes sacred. Not because it is already a prescribed sacred space, a church or temple, or a grove within the forest but through your intent, through your presence and your actions. Through the act of prayer you make the space around you sacred, through devotion you create a hollow that is filled by the Divine, by sacrificing, offering completely your inward nature to the Divine Presence that is formed, you provide yourself with the opportunity of being completely given that that you need and require in accordance with your highest will. By being mindful, open and receptive you provide the avenue through which the Divine may speak.

Go forward then in love and take our words of love with you. Be open to God's love, to the Divine Source and know that you are never alone. In perfect love, in perfect truth and trust, in light, I take my leave and leave with you my love.

URANIEL

✦ Guardian Angel ✦

The love of the Divine, God's love, is a force and power which is largely misunderstood. It is an energy which has a presence that is not independent from the Divine Source but is often comprehended as such by mankind. The Divine, as you know, is a macrocosm of the microcosm of man. Mankind perceives themselves largely as being whole and even though educated man acknowledges that they have parts of their own psyche which they are not consciously aware of or in touch with they still believe themselves to be largely whole and complete. A psychologist would have a different perspective. They would perceive mankind as being very segmented; divided into anima and animus, into shadow self and inner child, into conscious and unconscious and superconscious mind. They would perceive these separate aspects of the psyche as being quite independent of each other, very separate, very individual, finding expression through the consciousness of man in hidden ways but nevertheless dynamic and separated from what mankind would consider to be the whole. As this is with the microcosm of man so in essence it is with the macrocosm of the Divine. The Divine, though whole and complete, also expresses its individual components very individually and the love of the Divine is a presence and a power which can be experienced and seen as very separate indeed.

The love of the Divine is non-judgemental and unconditional in nature. This means that it is a force which does not demand anything in return for its presence. It is an abundant, limitless force and source of power. It is not dependent upon the actions of an individual, upon their past or their present, upon their culture or their social status but is continuous and eternal and infinite. It does not judge an individual as to whether or not they are worthy of its presence or its abundance. It acknowledges rather that all are one, that all are equal, by seeing all as being souls. It acknowledges that the experiences that the soul gathers through its incarnations are largely illusionary in comparison to the eternity of the soul's original being and although these experiences are valid, that they in no way, shape or form tarnish or touch the eternity of the soul and therefore cannot be compared in regards to whether or not the soul is to be considered worthy of the abundance of the Divine's love. All souls are worthy because they are souls, because they are divine.

God's love then finds many expressions. It is a force and power which has been described in many different ways. One of the descriptions used by the church is "Holy Ghost". The Holy Ghost has always been a mysterious thing. Various different religious bodies have considered the Holy Ghost to be an array of divine expressions ranging from the body of the Divine Source which enfolds all to the consciousness of God. But the truth of the matter is that the Holy Ghost is the body of the Divine's love. It is not the Divine's feelings, for the Divine does not have feelings in the way in which mankind does. It is more the emotional body of the Source, an emotional body which is abundant with love, with purity, with truth and integrity.

This love is in truth a little beyond mankind's complete comprehension but it can be held in parallel with some of the emotions that mankind experiences on a smaller level. The love of the Divine, the Holy Ghost, is joy and celebration in regard for the creation of reality and mankind. It is akin to the love that a mother has for the child that she carries within her womb. Not a desperate love, not a need or a hunger but an acknowledgement of the miracle that she has been party to. It is akin to the love that we experience for a surreal and abstract thing. Like the love that we have for spring or colours. Like the love that we have for weathers or flowers. A love which is not conditional, a love which is part of our preferences, part of the makeup of our character and personality. The Holy Ghost, the love of the Divine, can be held in comparison to pride, not in its negative connotation but rather in a sense of joy at what has become of a creation. It is akin to wonder and it is akin to love. It is a love affair with itself and its own creation.

In conditional love there is always an element of fear. Fear that the love will disappear or be defiled. Fear that the love will be lost. In the unconditional, cosmic love of the Divine, fear is absent, making love free and infinite. This love acknowledges that although within limited reality change is the constant and nothing is forever, there is something which rests beyond this. That in the unseen, unknown world of limitlessness, outside of the temporal laws of time, there is eternity and that within the creation of the Divine, within matter and within man, there is a little of the eternal which has always been and which will always remain. This awareness of the eternal takes away the fear of loss and enables love to be free, enables the love to be free because it allows that that is to be, to be.

Angels are an expression of God's love, of the Divine's love. They are an expression of the Divine's love for the universe and its maintenance and the completion of its purpose and they are an expression of the Divine's love for man, particularly Guardian Angels such as myself. Guardian Angels are expressions of the Divine's love for each and every person that exists. They were placed like a kiss into the cell born from the Divine's body that became a soul and grew within this soul as a part of this soul, as a blessing from the Divine, to guide this soul towards its fulfilment and eventual return to the Divine Source. This is the reason why occultists and metaphysicists have differed in regards to their perspective of Guardian Angels, some perceiving them as being very separate from the soul and some seeing them as being one and the same as the soul itself. We are in essence separate and yet the same. We were created by God's love for man to serve man as an intermediary between the soul of man and the Divine but we were born within the souls of man by God's placement of its love within the body of the cell of the soul itself. We are part of your higher consciousness and yet we are also an expression of the Divine's love for you.

Our duty and our task then is to steer you towards the completion of your destiny, to guide you towards the successful neutralisation of your karma, towards those people, places and situations that will facilitate this process. To the contribution of your gift in each and every lifetime, which can change, but which usually remains faithful to the thread that runs through your life which is connected to the archetypal nature of your soul's essence, sometimes known as "the soul's ray of incarnation" and also to enable you to learn, to guide you towards the learning that you need in order to be complete. As expressions of the Divine love we Guardian Angels, much like all other Angels, are unconditional and are non-judgemental. Our focus is upon you but we are not enamoured with you because of your good deeds or repulsed by you because of your dark actions. We see only the light of the Divine that burns within you, and everything else we acknowledge is a device for learning, an illusionary experience within the eyes of the Divine which does not mar the eternal within you.

In the fulfilment of our duty we are sometimes guided to steer you towards situations which you may experience as being painful. If these experiences will encourage you to grow in the correct way then they are deemed as being appropriate. This for some means that we are presences that they feel they cannot rely upon. It is true we cannot always be relied upon to make your life pleasurable but we can be relied upon to provide you with guidance which will ultimately be for the greater good of your entire being. We would never steer you towards anything that would cause you harm that you could not heal yourself from or towards a situation that would endanger you in a way which you could not cope with. This is beyond us because ultimately our essence is derived from the Divine's love for you and this, this primary motivation, overrides everything else which is part of our being.

We then have been with you since the first moment that you detached yourself from the body of the Divine and entered into limited space and time, since the very first incarnation that you ever knew, and will remain with you until the very last. We have been present at all of the births that you have known and all of the deaths and have strived to guide you safely into the light of the spiritual world and back towards the higher self, the soul. We have endeavoured to enable you to benefit from the wisdom of our experience, the wisdom of our experience of your lives, and always we have strived to steer you towards the greatest truth, the brightest light, the most appropriate and positive existence.

Our energy connects with you when you are in physical form at the point of the solar plexus centre. Often people are rather bewildered by this fact believing, understandably so, that our energy would be connected to one of the higher chakral points within your energetic body. The solar plexus point is akin to the energetic umbilical chord. of the physical form. It is to this point in the body that the astral form, the vehicle that you use for projected consciousness and journeying, is connected and because of this it is to this point that we are aligned when you are in body also, so that we may maintain a connection which will enable us to guide and steer you on a physical, conscious level as well as maintaining a watchful eye over your astral presence and the needs of your physical form. When you seek then to connect with us, it would be to this point that we would encourage you to focus your attention and bring your consciousness to and to seek with your mind's eye, with your imagination, from this point a glowing link of light, an etheric umbilical chord that will align and connect you to our being. This link is allegorical, it is not a tether that binds us to you but more a signal of energy that allows us to remain attuned, that allows us to find you. It is the point where our presence exists within that part of your soul which is present within your body. It is important always to bear in mind that although your consciousness often perceives us as being separate from you, we are in essence part of you and therefore found within you as much as we are found outside of you.

The following ritual then is a ritual of attunement. The Guardian Angel can be attuned to for guidance or protection or healing or general help. Although our concerns are largely for the greater good of your soul self and smaller queries and questions are better addressed to your spiritual guides, we will never shun a question but seek to steer you towards the answer directly, through your intuition or through an open dialogue if you are fortunate enough to have established such a thing or through omens and portents.

RITUAL

In a quietened room with a little music or silence, having burned a little incense and lit a candle in order to make the moment marked as being particularly spiritual, we would have you close your eyes and steady your breathing. Begin to centre your awareness in the solar plexus point of your body, becoming primarily aware of the physical sensation of this point within the form, of the way in which your clothes rest upon this area, upon the gentle rhythmic breathing, the sensations that affect this part of your physicality. Envision, imagine in your mind's eye, the solar plexus as a flower of golden yellow light, like a summer flower blazing with majesty and radiance, and see from the centre of this blazing flower of light a stream of energy like a translucent, effervescent, yellowy-white stream of light which flows out from the solar plexus into the space around you, connecting you to us.

Allow in your imagination our form to build, in accordance maybe with a description that you have already been given regarding the nature of your Guardian Angel or into a stereotypical image that you already have inside your mind. Try to keep your mind relatively open so that the Angel can impress upon your imagination some of its own particular qualities or rather the qualities that it seeks to express at this moment in time. Try not to have too many expectations in regards to how the Guardian Angel may appear before you. See them shining, smiling, arms outstretched, radiating God's love towards you. God's love is a flowing stream of pale pink light, shimmering and shining; a field of energy which you become more aware of as being part of the fabric of your reality and the fabric of your own being. It enfolds you, holds you as if it were a solution in which you had always existed, but it also flows through you and is part of you, your blood and your bone and your muscle as well as your thoughts and the feelings within your heart. As you focus upon this field of energy, this solution, it becomes more apparent and more powerful and the Guardian Angel steps forward and embraces you and the embrace is long and lingering.

The presence and the power of the Divine's love is infinite and miraculous. It can cure and heal and magnify. It can transform and clarify. It can lift and lighten and give love. Sit within this love, hold on to it, anchor it, be it, rest within it and then after a little while allow it to fade away. Take some time to re-centre yourself, to ground and protect yourself before you snuff out the candle and enter back into your ordinary reality. This communion with the Guardian Angel can, if you so choose, become a regular occurrence or may be something that you choose to do only when you feel the need for guidance or for the reassurance of the loving presence of God's love in your life. It can have miraculous effects and cannot be overused. It is a presence and a power which is indeed eternal.

END OF RITUAL

It is important to remember that God's love is not conditional. That God's love is not responsible for the actions of man or the actions of nature. It is important to acknowledge that God's love is like a veneer that covers everything. We would not blame the varnish on a piece of wood for the way in which the wood is used or treated and as such we must not blame God's love for the way in which mankind treats themselves or others or the way in which the Earth reacts to what is done to it by man. God's love is a solution, not in the sense of it being an answer but more in the sense of it being a force in which everything rests and resides. We are God's love for you and as such we are eternal and infinite. Remember this also; remember that you are never alone. In perfect love and perfect truth I take my leave and leave with you my love.

ARCHANGEL
◈ RAPHAEL ◈

The Angel of the Element of Air

I am Raphael, Archangel of the element of Air, guardian of the Eastern quarter, bringer of grace and flow. I am the Angel of the word, I am the Angel of song; I am the Angel of healing and of truth. I am the Angel of communication and this is my age. I am the Angel of thought and all those things that are created through this powerful, creative process of light.

I have come to speak of one of the many attributes that I am guardian and patron of, that of healing. Healing and health is a powerful preoccupation upon your planet. It is something which each and every one of you strives towards at some point in your life. Something that you are steered towards by the consciousness of your society, of your parents, of your peers, something which many hunger and crave for and something which many people battle to attain through illness, through pain and sorrow, through heartache, disease and the imbalance of body, heart, mind and soul.

In the spiritual community, the New Age community, at this moment in time, viewpoints have been held regarding the nature of illness which some find uncomfortable to digest. These viewpoints are close to the truth but there are aspects of them which are too dogmatic and too general to be applicable to the whole. In this discourse I hope then to set to rights some of the misconceptions regarding the nature of illness and those things that create it; the whys and wherefores of why humans experience illness and disease and the purpose that these things truly serve.

One theory within the New Age community is that all illness and disease is a manifestation of a deeper, more unseen root cause; an imbalance of mind and heart and body and soul, an external manifestation of the dis-ease of the unconscious. Some people believe that disease and illness is the unconscious mind creating and manifesting an illness in order to alert the consciousness to an unseen imbalance which exists within the subconscious and unconscious sections of the psyche. This, of course, to a certain degree is true but there are certain illnesses and diseases, there are certain imbalances within the body, which are not created from this point. Illnesses and diseases which we inherit from others, disorders and problems which are created as a result of other people's anger or foolishness or folly, problems which are genetic which we inherit not directly in this lifetime but as a part of our biological inheritance from a parent or ancestor also fall within the category of those problems which are not brought into manifestation through the unconscious mind. Of course there are always exceptions to the rule. Sometimes an unconscious imbalance steers the individual in an unknown and unaware way to encounter an illness through another person that will illustrate or bring to the conscious mind an imbalance which exists within the subconscious sectors of the psyche but in general, illnesses that are inherited or experienced in this way are not illnesses which have their root cause in this lifetime's imbalance.

Some of these illnesses and diseases can be karmic in origin and we are encouraged or guided towards experiencing those things that will bring about these inheritances because of karma that we have with a particular individual from whom we inherit the disease or problem. A person who attacks us in this lifetime or someone whom we inherit an illness from may be someone who we have wronged in a previous incarnation and who is being used in this lifetime to balance the imbalance of karma that exists between us. That is why even in these circumstances we must not be prompted to judge that individual who has caused our illness simply because we see them as being the origin of the problem that we encounter. In truth, we ourselves may be the origin of this problem, not in this lifetime but indeed within a former one. But sometimes the inheritance of these diseases and problems is simply circumstantial, which is not to say that they do not fulfil a higher purpose, because indeed they will and do but which is to say that we do not inherit them because of any unconscious manipulation or because of any karmic connection but simply because it is part of our unfoldment, our destiny, to experience this illness. The illness, the disease, the condition, provides us with a challenge, an opportunity for growth, for expansion and therefore our receipt of it is akin to a gift or opportunity that enables us to evolve, to progress, to transcend, to overcome the challenge and to move forwards on our spiritual journey.

The spiritual journey is not purely one which is to do with conscious transcendence or increased spiritual understanding. The spiritual journey is also about experiences, experiences which are located, found, here within this reality. These experiences can be emotional or purely physical or instinctive and reactionary but if embraced properly can encourage us to progress, to evolve, to expand in a way which we had not previously experienced. To value life more is an evolutionary experience. To recognise the value of love is another evolutionary experience, to recognise the folly of our former life and to reprioritise our journey another. To acknowledge that our life is not only for pleasing ourselves but also for a greater purpose, yet another spiritual opportunity for expansion and growth.

Most human beings who live upon the planet suffer from a blindness; an inability to see, to remember, to conceive that they have existed before, that this is one in a series of lifetimes that they are experiencing. They consider themselves only in the now and this has certain benefits for living life but it also prevents us from acknowledging our infinite nature, our eternity. It prevents us from seeing that disease or illness is part of a process of continued expansion. That it is not how we are always going to be. It is not how we have always been but is simply an experience along our journey, along our path, that enables us to see the world in a different light, through suffering sometimes, through pain, but also through priority, through immediacy, through the now that colours and changes our perception of reality in a way which can potentially be evolutionary and expansive.

People do not often pause to think, why? Why have they become ill? What is the lesson inside this experience? They concentrate on the solution, on clearing the problem, on getting better, and this is understandable. But often the only way to get better is to understand why the illness exists in the first place. Many people concentrate on the negative. They see the illness as a sign of imbalance, of bad karma, they see the illness as being an indication that they are out of alignment with themselves, whereas sometimes the illness is simply an opportunity to grow, to reappraise, to refocus, to recognise a certain truth, to become enlightened and is in no way, shape or form an indication of the individual's lack of goodness.

Many people are unhappy with the New Age perception

that illness is a manifestation of our higher consciousness' desire for us to grow, because they believe that this is in its own way a judgement. That the higher self is blaming them for their past life actions or for their actions in this lifetime and that the illness is a form of punishment, that the experience that brought the illness is a condemnation of their past. This is not true. Situations that we experience in life, however joyful or however dark, are opportunities for growth. Whether they are brought about by our own being or whether they occur because of the actions of another person's free will, the silver lining within every cloud is our opportunity to transform the negative into the positive, to transform the shadow into the light. This is not easy. The truth is that it takes more energy to be positive than it does to be negative. It is easy to be negative, to collapse into our pain, to experience our disease or illness, our problem, from the perspective of the victim or the ill person. It takes a great deal more energy to rise above our symptoms, to try and see where they are leading us, to transcend them, to transform them, to be healed. Many people who visit healers have no more energy left. They have exhausted all possible areas. No orthodox medicine can cure them. Their positivity has been exhausted and they seek a miracle. But a miracle can only be brought into being if the individual is willing to look at their problem, at the illness, at the disease and see the lesson, the opportunity, the challenge within it and to work with the healer by allowing the healer's energy to marshal their own force and to support them in their journey of self-transformation. This is why many people who visit healers have unsuccessful experiences, because by the time they journey to the healer they have no energy reserves left, they have no power to aid the healer in the healer's task and the energy that they draw from the healer brings them only to the surface of the water where they float and breathe but where they still do not have the capacity to lift themselves free. Healing is an act of co-opera-tion. The healer co-operates with the forces at their control to bring about realisation, restoration, balance, but it is also about the healee's co-operation with the healer, their will-ingness to be healed, to work with the healer's suggestion, to focus on their own transformation by exploring the nature of the illness and what it may mean to and for them.

There is another form of illness and disease which is much more widespread than many people would believe it to be and this is the illness that is brought about through our reac-tion to the imbalance of the world around us. Human beings are intimately connected to the world in which they live, through mind and spirit and heart but also through their body, not only in the obvious, physical way of reacting to chemicals in foods or in the air but in a subtle and ether-ic way too. We are one with the world around us, a micro-cosm of the macrocosm and as such we react to the pollu-tants and the irreverence that is paid our planet. For too long, mankind has forgotten the truth that the world around us is alive, it is a living entity, it is a consciousness that has a body and a spirit and a mind and a heart and a soul. The pollutants that have been pumped into the planet, the rav-aging of the Earth's resources, have diminished the Earth's holistic balance and that imbalance that we have created has been echoed within the imbalance that mankind has felt within their own form. Some, who have been linked to the Earth more powerfully in the past by the ways in which they have served it or drawn upon its power, spiritually speaking, are more susceptible to the Earth's imbalance than others but all in general are connected to the Earth's bio-sphere and as such are powerfully affected by the biosphere's imbalance.

Mankind has begun to realise that the world in which they

live has become polluted and they strive now to redress some of the harm that they have done. It is not enough at this moment in time but nevertheless it is a step in the right direction. When they heal the world around them they heal themselves. When they heal themselves they heal the world around them. But still there is much more to be done. What we can do is focus upon those areas in which we live. Take responsibility for those parts of the planet that we *can* affect. Oh yes, we can sign our petitions and send our money to those places that are in need but we can also focus upon our local environment and play our part in one way or another in healing and mending this environment, in ensuring that we are doing all that we can within our power to make sure that the space around us is not defiled or impure. On the physical level we can do this but also mentally, emotionally and spiritually we can send out our light into the environment in order to create harmony, focusing on those areas that we know may be in particular need. Places where there is a great deal of vandalism or litter, or where the etheric energy has become distorted by power plants or electric pylons or radio and communication masts, places that have been raped and pillaged, the quarries that exist and mines. The imbalance within the world is one which is not only brought about by the pollution of the environment, the destruction of the physical planet but also the traumatic affect that this has upon the planet's mental and emotional consciousness and therefore in sending out our healing to the world we must address this issue also and seek to restore the intimate connection that exists between us and the world, restoring the world's confidence in us and aligning the connection that exists between the subtle forms of the world's consciousness.

The final way in which I would speak regarding the nature of imbalance that exists within people and our planet at this moment in time is to do with integrity and truth. Integrity, truth, holds and binds the subtle bodies together, strengthening their covalent bonds, the bonds of energy that hold them in balance and alignment. The subtle bodies are different vibrationary fields which are constructs, projected outwards from the chakras, that enable us to think and feel and experience and express ourselves in certain ways here. They translate on to the physical dimension as our senses and also as our various forms of consciousness, our thoughts and our feelings. The subtle forms are distorted by a lack of integrity or truth that we hold inside ourselves. When we lie to ourselves or to others or to the world around us, when we deny truth, when we suppress it, when we delude ourselves or others, we place stress upon our subtle forms, we encourage them to enter into states of contrition where they pull against each other, creating distortions and warps within their harmony. This leads to imbalances which promote a lack of health, where we become ill because the distorting fields of our subtle forms allow certain illnesses to seep into us or create certain manifestations from within, which manifest finally into the physical body as problems within our own physical nature.

This is why it is very important that we are always truthful to ourselves, to others and to the world around us. That we maintain as best we can a conscious integrity, that we do not lie to ourselves, do not delude ourselves, do not hide or suppress but that we are always honest, open and truthful with ourselves and others. All of this we know may sound very complicated, the different things we need to think of and contemplate regarding our own illnesses and the illnesses of others. But it boils down to one single truth: illness is forged primarily to encourage transition, change, ascension, evolution and growth. Whether the illness is brought about by karma, through our relationship to the world, through a lack of integrity or through environmental factors beyond our control, it all encourages us to move towards a point of change and growth, of transformation, realisation and ascension.

RITUAL

The little ritual then that I would now provide is a general ritual that can be used for all healing upon others or upon the self. If there is an imbalance that the individual needs to work on consciously it will expose it, it will bring it to the surface. It will confront the individual with this truth. If it is, however, an imbalance that can be corrected without the need for the individual to confront anything, without the need for the individual to recognise any conscious imbalance, then it will facilitate this process also, though in certain cases and circumstances it is a healing that will need to be repeated several times in order to encourage a complete and successful rebalancing and cure.

It calls upon a particular vibration, a specific ray of light. It is an energy which comes from one of the higher spheres, from the Buddhic sphere, the sixth sphere. The Buddhic sphere is the sphere of reflection. It is also the sphere of challenge and confrontation. It is the sphere in which the perfect template of the Divine is held and reflected down towards mankind so that they may strive to grow into this etheric blueprint of perfection.

Make sure then that you will not be disturbed. Make sure that you are relaxed, warm, comfortable and calm. If you have a gold candle, then light it. If not, a white candle will suffice. Take a few moments to relax, breathing slowly and gently, calming and centring yourself. You may have some gentle music playing or a little incense burning if you choose; a high vibrational incense such as frankincense would be ideal. After you have relaxed for a moment, speak this prayer:

"I call upon the power of the Buddhic sphere; the light of reflection, the light of confrontation, the light of challenge, the light that will enable me to see the truth. Let this light now fall. Let it expose all that needs to be seen in order to facilitate this healing. Let it restore. Let it rebalance. Let it reorder. Let it illuminate the blueprint of my etheric perfection and overlaying this template upon myself, restore me to perfect health in mind, body and spirit. I ask these things in accordance with the Divine Will and the Divine Plan, so long as they flow in accordance also with my higher self and harm none. Let them then be so. So mote be."

Visualise a golden stream of energy. The golden stream or ray of light falls around you. It fills your body; it fills your aura; flows through your meridians and chakras and into your subtle forms. It aligns and corrects the imbalance that exists there but at the same time exposes and draws to the surface the nature of any imbalances that you may at this point in time need to redress. As the golden light falls and flows around you then keep your mind open. Allow thoughts to float into your consciousness. Acknowledge them. Do not dismiss them but simply witness them as they float to the surface of your mind. These thoughts may not immediately seem relevant but it is important to make a mental note of them so that you can re-explore them at a later point, as they may have hidden significance in regards to the nature of the illness that you experience.

After a little while change the focus of your visualisation. Visualise now two interlocking triangles which form a hexagram, a Star of David. A Star of David is a powerful symbol which represents the spirit and the soul co-joining together as one to create the essential self. It also represents the Merkabah, the light body vehicle which is also an ascension chamber, a focal point for energy which encourages the promotion of your perfect self. Focus on this simple two-dimensional image, the hexagram before you. See it formed of golden light, radiated golden light, acknowledge its perfection and its balance, contemplate its representations and its symbolic purpose. Hold the image for a little while in your mind whilst still entertaining any other thoughts that rise to the surface of your consciousness.

Finally, see, imagine or hold the intention that the hexagram is now the Merkabah that surrounds the body, a three-dimensional Star of David. If you are not someone who is particularly proficient at visualisation do not try to imagine this three dimensional construct but simply hold the awareness that this is now around you, that it draws energy into you, that it perfects and balances the energy that you already contain within yourself and that it harmonises your relationship to the world around you, the macrocosm, the Earth. That it enables you to restore the balance within your immediate geographical relationship whilst also strengthening the connection that exists in harmony between the world and you.

After a little while release all visualisation, take a few deep breaths and bring your consciousness back to the space of your surroundings. Open your eyes, snuff out the candle's flame and know that you have completed this opportunity for self-healing.

END OF RITUAL

This visualisation can be done on behalf of others during healing treatments. It can be done several times but it is always important, whether done upon the self or with others, to encourage them to speak about those things that have floated into their consciousness, as these things may in one way or another highlight those areas that exist within the psyche that need to be redressed in order to clear the imbalance that exists and that creates the symptoms within the physical form. This may take some interpretation as often these things may seem in no way connected to the illness, disease or problem that the individual encounters but with a little applied wisdom, connections should be seen and recognised and a course of action can be taken in order to work on these areas and bring them into greater alignment and balance.

Healing is a complicated area because there are so many different causes for disease, illness and problems of the mind, body, heart and soul. Many healers who enter into the healing practice do not contemplate the complexity of this area but rather practice blindly the healing art that they have been taught in a very automatic way. They often become confused when the healing that they seek to bring into being does not work but they would do well to contemplate some of the more complex causes rather than focusing only upon the cure. As I have said, successful healing is a co-operation between client and healer. It is not simply about bombarding the person with healing energy. It is about developing a mutual investigation into the nature of cause and dealing with the situation from the root level always.

In ancient days healers would labour long and hard within mystery temples and schools to understand these truths. Unfortunately, in this era of instant spiritual attainment, such mysteries are rarely contemplated by many who would call themselves "healer" and present themselves as such. There is a certain danger in such irresponsible healing practice which needs to be curbed if the New Age and spiritual community is to retain any dignity regarding its own claims as healers of the New Age.

Go forward then and contemplate the truths that have been outlined here. Practice this simple healing technique, work upon the imbalances that exist within your being. Begin your journey towards health and balance always from within. In peace and love and blessing I leave you with this light and love and take my leave.

Archangel
✦ Michael ✦

The Angel of the Element of Fire

I am Michael, Lord of Flame, Archangel of the South, master over the powers of passion, alchemy, transformation, perception and protection. I am the hero and warrior of the Divine. The force that was created to represent and champion all those who would seek a path of light that would take them through the shadows of their own mind and heart and those shadows also that exist in the world around them that are drawn to the light that they themselves radiate from the centre of their being. The shadows of doubt and fear, of opposition, challenge and despair. The shadows that exist as part of the integral fabric of our reality, the shadows that are part of who and what you are.

My message concerns the nature of protection. Its importance, the common sense that needs to be applied in regards to its application. The hows and whys, the wherefores, what can and must be done in order to aid and assist yourself as you progress and grow, as you develop, blossom and shine. But first of all, before we move into the mechanics of this procedure let us focus for a little while on exactly what protection is and why exactly we need it.

Protection is a vital part of spiritual practice. It is required because as an individual progresses spiritually and psychically their sensitivity to certain energies inside and outside of themselves becomes magnified. This sensitivity makes them vulnerable to certain energies which up until that point they had never had any need to be cautious or aware of. You see, there is a great natural protection in being "asleep", in being un-awoken to the spiritual and psychical worlds. Scepticism, non-belief, these things create natural psychic barriers to the darker and more shadowy world that exists inside and outside of the self, creating a natural protection and therefore eliminating the need to call upon powers or create forces that will repel negative energies from interfering with an individual's life. This is not the case with all forms of potential harm. Some entities and energies will penetrate even these strong natural barriers but for most a lack of belief is enough to provide them with adequate protection from energetic pollutants, from negative mental and emotional energy in an un-concentrated and undisciplined form and even from low-level elemental forces that may seek to do a person harm.

When we develop psychically or spiritually we raise our vibration. Some of us will awaken certain psychical centres within the body which will make us very sensitive to particular frequencies of energy of a psychical nature. Even those, however, who spiritually progress, not psychical in any way, shape or form, will nevertheless through their spiritual unfoldment become vulnerable to certain frequencies and areas of energy which may contain within them pollutants which could damage or interfere with that individual's quest for greater spiritual unfoldment and truth. Therefore anyone on the spiritual path, be it a path of psychical development or spiritual development or both, must acknowledge that there is need to call upon powers or to work with visualisations, rituals, talismans, in order to protect themselves from potential negative encounters.

Negative encounters come in a variety of different shapes and forms. Some are purely energy, energy which is a result of negative thought, which is a result of devices that radiate strong electromagnetic forces; x-rays and microwave energies, natural forces that rise from the Earth itself, these pollutant energies or energies which are simply disharmonious with the energy of the seeker, of those who journey towards enlightenment or spiritual awakenment. These energies will interfere with their progress, will harm their mental and emotional bodies, will damage their etheric form and disrupt their link to the realms of higher spiritual potential and consciousness. But there are also other forces which are more intentional, low-level elemental presences which have strayed into this dimension and which seek to sustain their own life by drawing life from others. Like tics or fleas these elemental astral presences attach themselves to people who carry light and feed off this energy, or feed from an individual's negative energies in the form of depression, anger, hate or fear and grow from these strong psychic currents. More people than you would care to imagine carry entities of this nature and more people than you would ever begin to comprehend are adversely affected by either these presences themselves or the way in which they are left by these presences when they choose to bail ship and move on to a person who carries a stronger energy, more potent life forces than the ones that they have just drained.

Of course, there are other forms of negativity that exist in the universe, darker entities and presences, demonic forces, and there are also powers which are less disciplined or focused but nevertheless powerfully negative in nature, forces which are beyond your comprehension, in truth. Forces which are more surreal in nature, less malignant but nevertheless whose vibration is not compatible with your own. And then there are those individuals on Earth who would direct consciously and with discipline their negative thoughts towards others in forms of psychic attack or cursing. Although the percentage of individuals who truly enter into these practices is still low, there are more now than ever before who are dabbling with these forms of black magick because more available than ever before are formulas that can be bought and employed to do just this. Therefore you see there is a great need for psychical and spiritual protection from the unintentional, natural, negative forces that we might encounter in our everyday as well as those elementals and negative powers that might exist in the world around us, who would seek to feed off our living life force or directly and purposefully interrupt our spiritual progression.

It is very important that we do not allow our fear to magnify the negative forces that we might encounter. We must never live in fear, particularly not of negative forces or presences that we might encounter. We must rather simply focus on the act of protection and not give mind to what we might encounter or what someone might be doing.

In order to protect ourselves then we can of course call upon our Guardian Angel, our spiritual guides, our totem animals or familiars or our patron Ascended Master or archangelic being. Such invocations would need to be done regularly each and every day, not because such presences need to be reminded but because the act of invocation anchors the energy that we are seeking and the energy that these presences desire to give us. We must never assume that one invocation will last a lifetime, not because our prayer has not been heard but because the act of prayer and invocation is in itself an act of anchoring the power that we seek. It is also important to take responsibility for our own protection and invoking every day in a disciplined fashion the protection that we seek *is* taking responsibility, even though we are calling upon a higher power to effect the protection that we need. Assuming that our guides or Guardian Angel, who want us to work for the Divine, will therefore take care of us is a presumption which is dangerous and egocentric. No individual on the planet, however great they may be, however evolved or whatever they do for Spirit is so important to be taken care of in such a luxurious and royal manner. Any high spiritual person should already understand that part of being an evolved and advanced personality is taking responsibility for one's own wellbeing, from the food that you eat to the rest that you take, to the protection that you summon to safeguard yourself.

Many people prefer the method of calling upon a higher power for protection because they fear that their own endeavours to protect themselves will not be strong enough. Calling upon a higher power is always advisable and if you are not particularly confident in regards to your link with your guide or Guardian Angel or with the particular master who is said to patronise the path that you walk upon then you can always call upon *my* protection to help. I am, amongst other things, the Archangel of Protection and can be called upon in all situations to aid people, places and situations by casting around them a protective circle of fiery energy to safeguard them and keep them well. Invocations to me, and indeed to all presences, however, must be done earnestly. They must not be recited as a form of rote but must rather be done in a concentrated and determined fashion with a great deal of intention. It is intention that makes the link and that anchors the power. Not the words that are used, not the poetry that is invented, not the Latin or Sanskrit but the intention behind it.

Certain formulas and certain power words contain vibrational keys which over time have built up thought forms that enable energy to be focused in very powerful and specific ways, but underneath it all it is the will of the individual that is the most important and powerful key. And so a simple prayer of protection such as "Archangel Michael protect me now" done with the right amount of determined, focused intention will have the same effect as any individual performing the more complicated "Lesser ritual of the banishing pentagram" or the complex visualisation of a merkabah star tetrahedron shield.

There are some who prefer to rely upon their own ingenuity in order to protect themselves and this is in no way looked upon darkly by Spirit but indeed rather admired. There are many different forms of protection that can be employed, from visualisations such as seeing oneself sealed in an egg of mirrored light or a cloak of violet energy to crystals that can be programmed and worn such as carnelian, tiger's eye, sugilite, amethyst and so on. Also herbs that can be burnt and waived around an individual within their auric field in order to coat them with a vibrational layer of protective power, such as lavender or sage. It is, at the end of the day, an individual choice depending upon the individual's tendency to be drawn to particular practices, which may in its own way be dictated by the past lives that they have had and also dependent upon their spiritual or religious belief.

No one protection is particularly more powerful than another but all protections are determined by the nature of the individual's focus, belief and sense of determination and connection with the power that they are employing. If an individual is connected to Angels then they must call upon Angels. If an individual is particularly connected to the mineral kingdom then why not use a stone talisman? If an individual has a strong affinity to herbs and oils then indeed use these to create your protective boundary.

A very powerful form of protection, however, that most people can employ is simply the raising of vibration. When we raise our vibration we lift ourselves above and beyond the negative energy that is being aimed at us. Imagine then that you are standing by a ladder and someone is aiming a gun at you, their aim is fixed and when they pull the trigger you will be shot. However, if you climb the ladder you will be out of the trajectory of their bullet and the bullet will go past you and miss you and you will be unharmed. This is the same principle as the raising of vibration. When we raise our vibration we lift ourselves above the trajectory of the negative energy that is heading towards us. We lift ourselves above its aim. Negative energy is by its very nature negative and low vibrational in nature, although negative energy exists on all the vibrational levels within those spheres that are governed by the limitations of this reality. The negative energy that exists in the higher spheres comes from negative entities which are of a higher nature and therefore although in time you may encounter these beings, in general negative energy that we may encounter here on the physical plane will be avoidable by raising our vibrations into these higher spheres.

Now the act of raising our vibration may sound complicated and daunting but in truth it is a very, very simple thing to do. All that we have to do is to think positive thoughts, happy thoughts, thoughts of peace and joy, thoughts of love and harmony, thoughts of happiness and glee. Focus on something that makes you happy; a person whom you love, something that makes you smile or laugh, a moment in time that you experienced in a very positive way, an image of beauty, an image of innocence, music that makes you feel joyous, liberated and freed, a colour that makes you feel uplifted. Anything that makes you feel positive, joyous, happy, content, at peace, fulfilled, uplifted. Any of these images, any of these thoughts, will raise the vibration. Not permanently but enough for a short space of time for you to avoid the negative energy that you may potentially be encountering.

Within your physical world a number of rules apply, physical rules but also universal laws. One of the universal laws is called "the law of challenge". This law states that any opposing force which is greater than the force that you yourself raise to oppose it will destroy the barrier that you have presented and have its effect of entering into your space and energy. It is this universal law, the law of challenge, which many people do not take into account when using protective devices which employ the creation of a barrier. Barriers created by visualisation, by tokens or talismans, by the calling on of higher powers, are adequate to stop particular negative forces which are aimed against them. But if the negative energy which is aimed against you is more powerful than the barrier that you have erected it will penetrate the barrier and it will penetrate you. A lot of defensive psychical postures then invest energy in creating a barrier, repelling the attack, shielding oneself from the onslaught. These protective measures are all well and good but they focus in an engaging way upon the negative energy that is directed towards you, which already diminishes your vibration by redirecting your energy and by engaging even in this conscious way with the negative energy itself.

The method of raising vibration does not focus upon the creation of a barrier. It does not focus on engaging the energy in any way, shape or form. In fact, it focuses on quite the opposite. Rather than acknowledging the negativity, thinking about it, engaging it, it focuses upon lifting your consciousness away from it. Focusing upon the positive, focusing upon the light, focusing upon something which makes you happy. By not engaging with the energy in any way you are not allowing your vibration to be diminished. You are not investing in creating a barrier which may be penetrated anyway but you are simply lifting yourself free from the situation. This then, we would say, is in our opinion by far the best form of protection: lifting the vibration, focusing upon your happy thought, removing yourself from the line of fire.

Of course, this requires, if the onslaught is perpetuated in any way, shape or form, you to maintain a high vibration consistently, which in this day and age is not always easy. The majority of psychic attacks are not perpetuating. Individuals who focus negative energy towards a person do it as an assault. One blast, one stream of negative energy which is sent out to the individual. Sometimes curses are created which can linger, which can hang around seeking out the person, waiting for their vibration to fall and opening or cracking their aura in order to enter into them but such curses are difficult to create and the majority of people do not have the know-how to do such a thing. Entities that might man an affront would be of a high nature if they were to consistently linger waiting for the person to dip into the level where they could be harmed. An entity that was seeking an individual in order to drain them would become very tired, very quickly, of waiting for the individual to dip down into their level and would very probably seek someone else. Therefore the method of lifting the vibration is a good one. It does not necessarily require for you to maintain a constant high but as a state of being it is a good state of being to try and cultivate more and more in your life.

We acknowledge that at this moment in time maintaining a positive attitude is not always easy. Your world is a very busy one and at times it is full of darkness. It is very easy to be pulled down into the lower vibrations by things that you hear on the radio, see on the television, read in the newspaper, people that you encounter in your everyday. But raising the vibration is also a pathway towards enlightenment, towards spiritual progression and evolution and therefore it is something each and every one of you must endeavour to do anyway if you truly seek to grow in spirit. Try to avoid those things that you know will make you feel down and depressed and sad. Don't read the newspaper; don't watch the news, make sure that when you do you are feeling positive and strengthened, that you are in a space of unconditional love or non-judgementalism. Try to confront those people who you encounter who treat or respond to you negatively with positivity. Don't fight fire with fire but fight it with water. If someone is aggressive be kind, if someone is hateful be loving, if someone is full of spite be full of gentleness and care. Such responses often dissipate such negative energy and leave you feeling much more positive for the outcome.

There is then one final thing that I would say regarding protection and that is this: individuals tend to think that as they ascend, as they grow in spirit, as they become more enlightened, more spiritual, they do not need to worry about the negative energies that they leave behind on the lower planes. This to a certain degree is true. There are energies in the lower planes that you will leave behind that you will never need to entertain or encounter again. Energies which are connected through the lower nature of their vibration to the lower planes that you have moved beyond. But as was said, in all of the varying different vibrational planes and planes of consciousness that exist within your limited universe there are always going to be areas of shadow. This is simply because that within the realms of your limited universe there operates a law known as "the law of polarity" that states that wherever there is light there must also be darkness. Indeed, as the quality of light is different in the higher planes the quality of darkness will be different too and sometimes it will take on a completely different form and be almost unrecognisable. In some planes the darkness is not so much external but more internal in nature. It emerges as fear, as doubt, as self-examination. It emerges as the challenges of our patterns, our tendency to repeat negative acts that have been impregnated into our mental or emotional body by our ancestors or our parents. Sometimes the darkness is not always belonging to others or sourced in elementals or demons but more the darkness that rises from our shadow self, from our id.

In regards to protecting ourselves from these forms of darkness we can raise our vibration but sometimes also it is best to embrace these shadows in order to transform them, in order to accept them, in order to dissolve them into our being. To recognise that these shadows, that this attack comes from inside ourselves and rises to be recognised so that we may move beyond it by working through it. In some of the higher planes the darkness is still external but it is more complicated, more powerful and it is always there to teach us, to guide us in a way, to show us a lesson that we need to learn. The darkness that exists in our universe, in our minds, is not purposeless. It has its own agenda which is the maintenance of its own existence by anchoring mankind in the material world and preventing them from achieving the ultimate goal which is unification with the Divine Source, individually and globally. But also the darkness, which is part of the Divine and part of the Divine Plan, serves a function and a purpose too and that is to edu-

cate us about ourselves, about our strengths and our weak-
nesses, our fears and our aspirations, about the patterns that
we need to clear in order to be liberated, about the challenges that we are set karmically and within this lifetime, to
contribute our gift and to learn from the world around us.
It is important that you understand that the darkness is not
an aimless creature, it is not without function or reason but
that it serves a valid task, which is often to educate and promote enlightenment and growth.

The final thing then that I would leave you with is a prayer.
A prayer and invocation to me that you can use to call
upon my protective energies should you so need. In the
higher levels you can use this prayer to invoke my presence
from within you rather than externally, which is how you
might use the prayer on the lower levels. As we are all one,
as we have all been created by the Divine, as the universe is
macrocosmic, microcosmic and holographic in nature, then
everything that exists outside of ourselves also exists within us too. Internal invocation relies upon recognising this
fact and drawing the powers that exist outside of ourselves
through us from within. It is a very powerful form of invocation which can be used on the inner planes and when we
have risen to higher levels of consciousness and understanding.

PRAYER

"I call upon the power and the presence of the
Archangel Michael, the Archangel of the South, the
Archangel of the element of Fire. Hero and warrior of
God, hear my prayer. Shine forth and shield me, protect
and guide me, be my champion and safeguard me as I
walk upon my path of light. With your sword of flames,
with your wings as shield, beat back all darkness and

misunderstanding. Beat back all that that seeks to obscure my way. That seeks to pervert my word. That seeks to veil my truth, to pollute my integrity. Shield my mind, shield my heart, shield my body, shield my spirit and my soul and through this shielding set me free. Archangel Michael, I ask these things of thee, let them then be so, so mote it be, amen."

END OF PRAYER

Take then this prayer and go in peace and use the words of wisdom contained here wisely and well.

ARCHANGEL
✦ MICHAEL ✦

The Angel of Perception

The second communication that I bring forwards is not in my capacity as Angel of Protection or guardian of light but rather in my capacity as teacher. For the element of fire is also the element of perception, amongst other things. It is the light that burns in the brow, that cuts through the darkness of illusion and illumines truth. It is the power to recognise and realise and see and it is indeed this very art and skill that transforms the world around us, that enables us to rebirth the world through our new perception of its truths. The particular truth that I have come forward to speak about is a truth concerning the nature of Angels and their direct and intimate connections with mankind, with the souls of man and in the bodies of man, as Watchers and Nephalim souls.

Let me begin then by briefly defining the term "Watcher". In certain biblical texts the term "Watcher" is used for an Angel who takes on human form. In the Gnostic bible the Watchers were said to be Angels who fell to Earth and interacted directly with mankind as initially their teachers and guides and latterly their lovers, producing strange hybrid children known as "the Nephalim". Watchers were considered to be Angels who had lost their way, who had fallen to Earth and whose behaviour was considered to be less than divine. They were not usurpers to the Divine's throne or crown but rather misguided beings, divine and supernatural in origin but dark in their inclination. They were considered to be careless and un-thoughtful, unloving beings who were rampant and out of control. Of course, this is not true. Angels have never adopted human form by manifesting for themselves a body. On occasion Angels can create a physical countenance in order to directly interact with mankind but these constructs are temporary and only brought about in miraculous circumstances to avert disasters or influence man in a specific and powerful way. These are exceptions, which only occur in accordance with the Divine Will and the Divine Plan. Angels have never and never will create forms for themselves on Earth. But indeed, what some Angels have done is incarnated into a human form which has been created in the usual way.

Angelic incarnation only occurs for lower angelic presences. Higher angelic forms and frequencies, Archangels and Collectives and so on, cannot confine the great body of their energy and consciousness into a single human cell. These Angels would perform incarnation as a form of aspecting, which is sending a part of their essence to create a new higher self which will then operate independently of them, having been formed from their energy, and incarnate as a normal soul would, the result being that the incarnation is an aspect of the archangelic presence, a descendant of this presence, a relative of it, a soul formed from its essence and vitality but not the same thing. Angelic aspects incarnate in much the same way as lower angelic forms do and are subject to all the same limitations, difficulties and problems but also have all the same powers, capabilities and uniqueness, their archangelic ancestry, if anything, giving them slightly more than their relatives who are from the lower levels of the angelic continuum. These beings then, incarnate Angels and incarnate archangelic aspects, would be known as "Watchers", Angels which have taken on human form, though this term, in this particular period of time, is practically obsolete.

The Nephalim then are not those beings who are brought into manifestation through the union of an incarnate Angel and an incarnate human, as the child of two such people could very easily be human in nature. Simply because an incarnate Angel has contributed to the manifestation of a body does not necessarily mean that the soul that will inhabit that form will be angelic. The body itself that has been co-created by the incarnate Angel will contain some of the angelic resonance but this angelic influence will be minimal and therefore not particularly noteworthy. No, Nephalim souls are something quite different. A Nephalim soul is a process whereby an angelic force contributes some of its own essence and energy in order to create a higher self, a soul, which is brought into creation through the contribution of a human soul energy too. A Nephalim soul then is a hybrid soul, a soul brought into manifestation and creation by angelic and human souls' interaction. Human souls and angelic souls being born from the Divine have the capacity to co-create in accordance with the Divine's wishes and the Divine Plan and have the power to bring other souls into manifestation, the Nephalim soul being one such soul that can be born.

Nephalim souls have free will, unlike angelic beings, and yet Nephalim souls contain certain angelic traits, energies and powers, which are much more to do with their angelic parent than their human one. They are often very empathic incarnations. They have great light, they have unusual and extraordinary psychical and spiritual abilities and powers but above and beyond all else their uniqueness is in their capacity to hold and contain energy. The incarnate spirit of a Nephalim soul has a powerful resonance, a combination of mental and emotional divine energy, of God and Goddess force. This enables them to become a perfect vehicle, a perfect vessel or channel to hold or contain extraordinarily powerful forces. Nephalim souls have been used since the beginning of time to be channels for the spiritual hierarchy or to embody spiritual forces of great power; Cosmic Ascended Master presences and high angelic forms, to be the voice piece, to be the body through which these energies will for some time benignly possess the physical form of the Nephalim soul in order to experience and contribute to the Earth.

This capacity to hold and contain energy means that the Nephalim souls often find themselves in positions as teachers, oracles, guides, healers, miracle-workers of one form or another, or simply anchorage points for great light, peace, love and truth. Many of the Nephalim souls on Earth have in the past been Lords and Ladies of Order, human beings who have held the power of Order on the planet in order to sustain the balance between light and darkness here. Nephalim souls are not always conscious of their origin and may simply consider themselves to be human like anyone else. They may live very ordinary lives and never have any conscious spiritual thoughts. Unconsciously they will carry the light that they as a vessel have been filled with or aligned to and bring that light into every section of their life, to every person that they meet, to every place that they visit, holding and anchoring the power. Some of the Nephalim, however, are conscious of their angelic origins, of their ancestry, are even conscious of the nature of the Angel who contributed to the creation of their soul. The nature of the Angel of course will dictate the resonant frequencies of the angelic components of the Nephalim's creation and create a specific resonant attunement that will enable them to hold or contain certain frequencies of energy.

As an example, let me use myself. I, the Archangel Michael, have in the past created with human souls Nephalim souls to be vessels to hold energies which are in resonance and alignment to my own element and power, to hold energies of light and enlightenment, of awakening, of a catalytic and alchemical nature, of a protective nature, of warrior forces. The Nephalim that *I* have created, *my* children who have existed upon the Earth, have been teachers, guides, leaders, warriors, protectors. They have led the way by holding great strategic consciousness and understanding of the nature of mankind and what needs to be done in order to restore balance, even if that means using force or controlling others in order to affirm positivity through war. The Nephalim that I have created have brought great light and understanding to the world of man by holding consciousness within their own consciousness that has guided them to unveil and reveal hidden truths. The power of fire, of light, of my element has burnt brightly in the vessels that have held other great forces of a similar octave or energy, which have been used to banish the darkness of your world.

Why then have I been asked to bring forward this guidance at this moment in time? The truth of the matter is that there are more Nephalim souls upon your world than there have ever been before, partly because your world is in a state of crisis and partly because your world is approaching a critical time of change. This critical time requires light in order to ensure that the world will move towards its own re-creation rather than its own self-destruction. Nephalim souls holding light and truth of a powerful nature can contribute to this. Because Nephalim souls have free will they are not restricted as other Angels are in regards to seeking to convert the consciousness of mankind. Of course, the Divine does not particularly favour converts or converters but if an individual in all passion desires to expand the consciousness of another with their truth, not out of a desire to control but out of a true desire to liberate consciousness, then this does not oppose the Divine Plan but strengthens it. Some of the Nephalim on your world at this moment in time are anchorage points for power and light and energy to try and maintain a fragile balance upon the planet whilst the planet restores itself and some are used to enlighten, to teach, to guide, to shine a light and show the way.

Many of you reading this book are Nephalim souls and therefore I have come to expand this concept so that you may begin to recognise the true nature of your being and through this recognition be liberated and through this liberation be more true to your own nature and your own purpose for being. The following description then is a generalised attempt to explain a little as to what it is like to be one of the Nephalim. It might be tempting to read this description and believe that you yourself are one of these beings but let me add with all haste that simply because an individual is a Nephalim soul does not mean that they are particularly evolved, enlightened or advanced. They can accrue karma like any other person can and they will need to ascend in the usual way to become enlightened by liberating their essential self and eliminating the conditioned patterns that have been forged in their consciousness throughout all of their previous incarnations by the societies, cultures and parents that they have lived through.

There are no easy steps that can be taken simply because of this descendency. Therefore think carefully when reading this description and make sure that you are recognising this as a truthful description of yourself not out of any egocentric desire to be special but because there is a genuine resonance with these words. Enlightenment is all about being true to oneself. If we, in our attempts or endeavours to do this, delude ourselves further by wanting to be something special, something that we see as being special and we are truly not that thing, then we are doing ourselves and our spiritual path a great disservice.

As I have already mentioned, Nephalim souls are usually very empathic, very sensitive beings, quite attuned to the emotional radiations of people and their world around them. They may often find it difficult to balance their empathy in early life and this can lead to complications and problems. They will carry a certain amount of the angelic tendency to be androgynous in nature and therefore may find themselves challenged in regards to easily fitting into a definition of sexual gender. They may be more psychically sensitive and mediumistic in nature than most. They will find that if they pursue mediumistic development and healing development they have the capacity to embody and transmit vast and powerful amounts of energy of great vibrational frequency and array and they will find mediumistically that they have the capacity to soar up the vibrational scales in order to access high frequencies of wisdom and truth.

They may experience large periods of their life where they feel distinctly unlike themselves, where they feel almost as if their body is being shared with another presence, where they are being led by another consciousness, which is not their own true nature. They may find themselves guided to places or people to say things, to teach and speak on subjects which in truth they feel they have no great knowledge of. They may feel as if their life has a very specific function and purpose, as if they are continually being guided to bring forward teaching or to bring forward guidance, to illuminate or heal in a very specific way. They usually have above average amounts of energy and light, which attracts many people to them, people of the dark as well as people of the light, and they often too feel a strong and yet un-definable link and connection to the Divine, a sense of being a priest or priest-ess to this presence, a sense of being a bridge through which this presence can operate, commune and communicate with mankind. They will have a holy sense and possibly a sense of obligation. They will have a sense of wanting to do good and often a great sense of justice too.

Simply because one is a Nephalim does not mean that their life will be charmed or rosy. They will have to work hard at opening themselves up to the energies that require to work through them and at grounding themselves sufficiently in order to be an effective conduit through which this light may pass and they will have to in all other ways live out their life as a human, though certain elements of their exist-ence may be charmed or blessed. If they flow in accordance with the true pull of their existence they will find that things will go very well for them indeed but if they try to enforce their own will on to situations which they know inside are not meant to be for them, then things will become stagnant and difficult. They have free will and therefore can choose to align themselves to this sense of flow or not but there is also a part of them which has been created to fulfil a function and a purpose and deep down inside they will know this to be true.

In the ancient Gnostic texts the Nephalim were described as giants. The Nephalim *are* giants on an energetic level but not in physical form. They were described as rampaging, powerful hybrids, monsters who would create chaos and destruction, who had ravenous appetites. It is true that the Nephalim carry great power and because they have free will they can choose whether or not to use this power for the light or the dark. In the past when people encountered the

Nephalim they were frightened of them because of the enormous light that they carried inside themselves and the reckless way in which they could choose to use it, but the Nephalim are not to be feared. They are to be simply acknowledged as another part of the rich tapestry of the Divine's creation.

The final part of my message is not particularly about the Nephalim but more about the nature of God's creations. All are equal in the Divine's plan, all have a role and a function to play; all are part of the clockwork. No one person or soul is considered to be more important than any other, irrespective of the plane or dimension from which they have originated. Mankind would do very well to remember that this is so. Envy of another person's origin is ridiculous and inappropriate, as each and every person is essential for the Divine Plan to will out on Earth. Remember this then. Each and every one of you is unique and important, needed here by the Divine in order to participate in the unfolding of the divine world.

Take then this knowledge with you and use it wisely and well for yourself and for others. I for my part leave you in love, truth and light.

ARCHANGEL
GABRIEL

The Angel of the Element of Water

What is often forgotten is that the formation of your universe did not begin with the physical kingdom but began higher in the seven spheres, crystallising as the energy and intent of the Divine's desire to bring into manifestation physical reality fell in vibration until it finally found manifestation in the space and time that you have come to know as your reality. What is also often forgotten is that we Angels have existed since before the beginning of time, created in order to help facilitate the process of creation and then later given smaller tasks to focus our intention and our light upon. When the multiverse was being created it was given to me, Gabriel, to focus over the astral sphere, to ensure that the formation of this dimensional reality and consciousness occurred in accordance with the will of the Divine. The astral sphere is a mirror of the physical dimension, it is the second sphere and it is the blueprint, the shadow, the-fore echo of the physical world in which you live. As some of you may know, the seven spheres, which include the physical sphere, your universe, lead upwards towards the Divine. Each sphere is subdivided into seven realms and between each sphere seven realms exist also. My discourse is not to explain the nature of the seven spheres, not even to go into detail regarding the seven sublevels of the astral planes, but rather to talk more generally about the nature of the astral worlds over which

I preside and their relevancy and connection to your physical dimension in the here and now.

Much has been said about the astral planes and mankind's
ability to journey to them through projection. In recent
years, channels have brought forward messages saying that
the astral planes would disappear as your physical world
ascended into higher frequencies and vibrations. Although it
is true that at some point in the future, if all flows in accordance with the Divine Will and your universe ascends, that
the seven spheres will gradually merge, becoming one,
enabling Earth to rise to heaven and heaven to descend
towards Earth, this situation at this moment in time has not
yet occurred. It is true, efforts have been made to clear some
of the lower levels of the astral kingdoms, the levels in
which the earthbound reside, though these planes belong
more to the first sphere than the second, even though they
are often referred to as being astral in nature. A purge has
taken place on your Earth to clear away those who are lost,
not only the earthbound spirits who have not managed to
find their way home to the spiritual world after death but
also those astral-dwelling entities which for one reason or
another have become stranded in your sphere and do nothing more than seek their way home, back to their native
dimension. These beings have fallen through windows and
pockets, tears within the fabric of the realities, that have led
them to this plane with no intention of being here, a plane
that is alien to them, where they seek only to survive whilst
they try to journey home. Often these entities are simple
beings who feed off energy in order to thrive, (their function in the astral worlds is to clean and clear away those
energies that sometimes seek to pollute it). In this dimension these parasitic entities can cause problems when they
attach themselves to individuals in order to survive by
draining off their negative energy and sometimes also their

positive light. Their intention is not malevolent or bad but simply instinctive and natural. In their home dimension they are fulfilling a valid function, here they are vampirising those who have great power, great darkness or great light.

The wounds and holes that exist in the veils that separate the kingdoms have been caused by a variety of things, energies that are now being haphazardly produced by mankind which unbeknownst to them are causing damage in the finer worlds: electromagnetism, radiations, microwave and x-ray technology and so on, as well as those energies that are being created by mankind purposely in order for them to journey through the dimensions and conquer the boundaries of time, experiments which have been taking place since the early 1900s in your history but which are still largely unknown to the populace of mankind. There are things that can be done, that are being done by both those who exist here in the physical dimension and those who reside in the finer dimensions too, to mend these rents and tears in the fabric of reality, and my brothers and sisters in the Cherubim and Seraphim will speak of those things that can be done to heal these wounds later, some of the wounds themselves being caused not only by these mechanical radiations but by the disharmonious emotional radiations of mankind that are generated through unjust action and endeavours which are brought into being that oppose directly the will and virtuous nature of God.

The astral planes then are a mirror, they are like a lake that exists above the sky, they reflect that which takes place here in the physical dimension and they also reflect on to the physical dimension those things that are meant to take place here. They are used to bring into manifestation the desires and wishes of the spiritual hierarchy and the Divine Source and they are used by mankind to bring into manifestation *their* dreams and desires too. Of course, in certain subsections of the astral realms there are inhabitants that are more complex and civilised than those astral beings that I have already mentioned. For indeed, it is within the astral kingdom that the elemental races reside, having largely removed themselves from the physical dimension and choosing now to exist in the astral planes, where they continue to watch over those responsibilities that were placed in their care by the Divine Source at the beginning of time concerning the Earth.

As some of you know, the elementals fled to the astral planes a long, long time ago when the rise of the Christian religion caused them to be focused upon as expressions of Satan rather than the natural inhabitants and manifestations of the divine consciousness of the planet. Choosing to weave a great spell, the elementals lifted themselves into the astral worlds that run parallel to the physical dimension and erased their existence from the memory of mankind, remaining only in the memories of those sages, mystics, priests and priestesses, wise men and women who were attuned to the powerful magickal nature of their world.

The astral sphere then is a complex sphere of interrelating energies, it is a place for manifestation, it is a place of communication and connection where the will of the Divine imposes its concentration so that it may bring forward its omens, its signs and its portents and its messages into the dreams, meditations and physical lives of the spiritual seekers. It is a place where the past, present and future intersect, it is a place where truth can be revealed and understanding known. But in much the same way as the astral sphere reflects the higher spiritual virtues and inherent powers of mankind it also reflects mankind's confusion and their deceptive nature, and some of the lower levels of the astral kingdoms are planes of illusion. The spheres are complexly connected to the consciousness of man. They are dimensions it is true; other kingdoms, other countries within the multiverse but they are also microcosmically found within mankind as different states of consciousness that they can enter into, that they can attune their awareness to. There is a part of every living being who exists upon the Earth in each of the seven spheres and when an individual attunes their consciousness to the sphere it is to this part of themselves that they connect in order to gain awareness of that plane. Astral projection in essence then is not projection at all but attunement to the astral body that resides already within the astral kingdom. The level in which the astral body resides, as with the other bodies that exist in the other seven spheres, is dependent upon the vibrational nature of the individual and will rise or plummet depending upon their progression or lack of it in this lifetime.

In the lower planes of the astral kingdom messages and truths are distorted, guidance offered and given becomes confused. The lower levels of the astral kingdom represent the unconscious mind of mankind and they are a jumble of thoughts and feelings and impressions, of emotions, of concepts and truths. They are a storehouse of mental images, understandings; they are the junkyard of the astral planes where all thoughts and feelings find manifestation. If an individual is attuned astrally only to this level of the astral sphere then impressions or messages that they receive will be contaminated by this jumble and they will receive the messages falsely, heavily contaminated, twisted, not only by their own consciousness but also by the impinging consciousness of those people around them. This is why channels who are connected only to this level will sometimes bring forward information of greater clarity than other times, depending solely upon the individuals who exist in the space around them. Also it is possible when a channel is attuned only to this level that they will not communicate with a genuine presence at all but rather with a masquerading thought form or a negative entity which has assumed the shape of the presence that the seeker is aiming to connect with. Mediumship, clairvoyance and channelling therefore is at times a dubious and dangerous pursuit and it is very important that the medium, psychic or channel endeavours to clear themselves and to raise their vibration before they attempt any form of communication with higher entities.

This also falls within the domain of my keeping and this is why I have brought forward this message for you, to provide you with guidance on how you might utilise my energy and power to clear yourself. Irrespective of the nature of your power, of your connection or link, the following guidance can be useful in clearing yourself time and time again of mental and emotional debris, of impressions, of pollution, of negativity that you have become saturated in by being exposed to certain people, certain places or certain situations, by thought forms and emotional feelings that rise up within you as a result of external stimulus, by energies that you may encounter in physical locations that you will journey to. This simple exercise of purgence and clearing is very powerful, very ancient and very strong, drawing upon archetypal symbols that have been utilised since the dawning of time.

RITUAL

Begin by seating yourself comfortably. Ensure that you will not be disturbed. Take the phone off the hook, dim the lights in the room, light a candle if you will and burn a little incense, all simply to relax yourself and to suggest to the self that you are entering into a state of meditation. Close your eyes. Breathe slowly and gently and relax. Bring your focus and your attention to your heart centre and as you breathe see and acknowledge that the prana that you absorb causes the heart chakra to blossom and bloom. The golden fragments of prana in the air, fed through your intention into the heart, cause the heart to open outwards like a rose. The chakra vibrates and pulses with its own gentle pink radiance and light and as you continue to breathe, the power of the pink light becomes stronger and more pervasive.

Now see with your mind's eye that the rose, the bloom of your heart centre, is held within the cup of a chalice, within the bowl section of a chalice that forms inside yourself. The bowl is large, wide, deep, the stem of the chalice strong, its base broad and secure. You may see the chalice differently, it may appear to each person who utilises this visualisation in a different metal or mineral or material. It may be intricate and decorated or simple and plain. The chalice represents the nature of your spirit, of your consciousness, that part of you that is the window and aperture through which the light of your soul shines. Do not become disturbed if you notice that your chalice is battered or warped or dirtied and polluted. If this is the case then this exercise will help in clearing this too, though primarily the exercise is focused upon clearing and aligning the mental and emotional subtle bodies of the energetic form.

Now imagine and see that from high above, a cascading waterfall of glittering light falls from the air above your head and pours down through the crown, down the etheric spine, the central energy channel, into the flower held in the bowl of the chalice, into the chalice itself and around it. The water is illuminated with light, it is powerful and clear and bright and shining. It vibrates with strength and energy. As the chalice fills the water overflows. It flows through the meridians of your body, through the blood vessels and veins, it passes along the energy channels and is distributed by the whirr of your chakras, like water shaken from the blades of a windmill. It flows over muscles and organs, around and through skin, saturating and soaking all, the water imbued with the light of your own heart centre, the light of your own intent which is to be cleared and cleansed. As the water flows around you and through you it soaks into the deep earth beneath you where is it taken away and transformed into light by the Mother. It washes you clean and clear of negative emotional energy and negative mental thought forms, it purges you of negative presences that may have attached themselves to you, of shadows and impressions and projections that may seek to do you harm. As you sit beneath the powerful, invigorating waterfall that comes directly from my heart you are cleansed and purged, energised and invigorated, filled with light and life.

Finally, as the waterfall stops flowing you begin to see another impression within your heart. The chalice and the flower give way and are replaced by the satellite of the moon; the moon is round, full, silvery and bright. It shines and shimmers with a perfectly reflective light. It shines with the light of your soul which falls down upon you from above like the sun emerging after the rainstorm. The light is gentle and pervasive, it moves through your body, it passes where the water has been, calming the storm of cleansing and replacing it with gentle tranquillity and peace. It replenishes the energy that has been lost, replacing the negative energy that has gone with positive energy that now sustains and nurtures. Your whole energy body is aglow with silver light and you are filled with this incredibly bright and powerful vibration.

In this moment you may find that you receive guidance; that those things that were unclear to you are now clear, that your concerns regarding connections that you had made are now revealed as either being true or false. The silver light enables you to connect to a higher realm within the astral sphere where you are connected to guidance that comes from the hierarchical realms of Spirit, that enables you to see the omens and portents of the Divine and to reconnect with your synchronicity, the strands of your life purpose and path. After a while let this visualisation go and breathe slowly and gently, bringing yourself back to this reality, giving yourself time to ground and centre yourself before you return to the normal tasks of your day.

END OF RITUAL

The astral plane then is a jumble of many different things, as is the consciousness of man. Some of its realms are secure and powerful, like the realm of the elementals, whilst other levels are confused and chaotic. It is an intermediary sphere which means that it is necessary for many things to find their way here onto the Earth to be manifested and to be received as consciousness, inspiration and ideas. As the consciousness of mankind clears so will the astral plane become more whole in its balanced and calm state. The clearing that is being done on the astral planes is not only to move on the earthbound souls or to rescue the lost inhabitants of the astral sphere but also to cleanse and purge the negative and confused thought forms that have become lodged in the lower levels of this sphere that are a result of mankind's confusion. As more work is done by Spirit and man to clear this plane, so too will in reflection the consciousness of man become more bright and less contaminated by their confusion, by their history, by their assumptions and their deceptions, lies and untruths and more will they become the reflective lights of their higher selves, the Divine, the God Source.

The final thing then that I would say is this. My power ranges in many different directions. I am the Angel of birth. I am the messenger. I am the inspirer of psychical development and the intuition. I am the bringer of emotional healing and I am a teacher of the heart but I am also the custodian of the dreamtime realms which each and every one of you enters into when you sleep. The dreamtime realm is used as much as all the other realms are in the astral planes in order to pass on truth; truth from the higher spheres and truth from the divisions of your own subconscious mind, to clear and purge you of unwanted and unnecessary thoughts and also to impart to you guidance from your spiritual guides and patrons in the Ascended Master and angelic realms. The purgence that I have given to you as a gift can be used before you sleep, to help inspire deep sleep, to wash away thoughts that will bar you from entering into this realm. Sleep is important, not only because it provides you with an opportunity to learn and be filled with knowledge, light and truth but also because it is essential for the spirit to reconnect with the soul in this unconscious state in order to sustain the spirit's continued existence in the body on Earth. Only those who have achieved attunement and connection to their higher self, their soul, in a perfect and enlightened way need not sleep but all others most definitely do need to.

You may then wish to try this exercise before you sleep but add a simple extra visualisation to it. At the end, when you have been filled by the moon's reflective light, hold the intention of wanting to connect with your dream totem animal. An animal may present itself to you. It will usually be an animal of an aquatic nature though it may be a bird that rests and swims within the water too. This animal is your dream totem. It may present you with a name or simply an image but once you have seen it and felt it you can call it to you and rely upon it as your guide in the astral worlds. It is a creature of the astral planes whose purpose is to guide and protect those who wander into these spaces but these creatures will take on the forms that are more familiar to those who enter into these realms, forms that come from their own world and they will ally themselves to particular individuals, coming to their summons and aiding them, whether they enter into the astral planes through conscious meditation or sleep. They can aid in bringing answers to questions, in bringing about the manifestations of desires or help resolve subconscious issues that need to be cleared from the deeper aspects of the mind. The shape and form of the dream totem will of course have some bearing upon the nature of your work in the astral realms and interpretation of the dream totem's energy can be done using the usual means of discovering the medicine or magickal qualities of the animal in question.

These are powerful times, when the consciousness of mankind and the energy upon your planet is shifting and changing. It is important now to begin to comprehend the mechanics of your universe and to work with Spirit to help in clearing the way for the transitions and changes to take place. The astral plane is very close to your dimension, it has become polluted by your existence and now needs to be cleared. The clearance of the astral plane will aid in the furtherance of mankind's progression and evolution. One of the things then that you may decide to do regularly, maybe in a group or simply on your own, is to bring the Violet Light into the astral plane, to take it with you as you journey into sleep or to project the Violet Light into the astral planes as you project your consciousness there too. To ask when you call upon the purgence of my power to be used as a conduit through which this purgence and the purgence of the Violet Flame may be breathed into the astral realms also so that you may play your part as a medium to this clearing.

The universe was not always as it is and will not always be as it is now. Change, the only true constant, forces everything forwards, forces everything to evolve and the seven spheres are subject to this change as much as the physical dimension is. But in order for these changes to occur we must work hand in hand at clearing the spaces that will be one day merged together as one and at taking responsibility for the pollution that we sometimes cause and bring. Taking responsibility for your world and the worlds that they touch upon is part of spiritual growth and evolution, is part of recognising that you are a co-creator within this divine plan and capable of healing that which your ancestors have damaged.

Go forward then in truth and love, take the wisdom from our words and use them well. Hand in hand we can recreate our world in love and peace.

ARCHANGEL
✦ GABRIEL ✦

The Angel of Annunciation
A Christmas Message

I am the Archangel Gabriel, Archangel of the West and Water, Archangel of dreams and seas, Archangel of the oceans and grace and flow. To many I am the Archangel of birth, because it was I who was instructed to bring the message of Jesus' birth to Mary. But in truth my affiliation and connection to the powers of birth began a long time ago in ancient Atlantis when, as patron of the royal family of water, it was my duty to instruct the priesthood of this royal family's cast as to the mysteries and ancient truths of birth in the spiritual and physical planes, creating on Earth the first midwives of your world.

I come forward in order to speak in part of birth but also of messages and messengers. For this period of time in your year is a time when Angels have been hailed and recognised and are thought of more strongly than any other time throughout your year, because of the part that Angels played in bringing forth the message of Jesus' birth and because of the way in which this is remembered and celebrated at Christmas time. Angels exist and have existed since the very beginning. Extensions of the Divine, we have always been entrusted with the care of man and of your world and often sent forth to the planet Earth in order to pass on mysteries and truths of great divinity and power that would aid mankind in not only their sustation but also their continued evolution. We were the original teachers of those arts and practices that you have now come to know as magick, philosophy, astrology, geometry, numerology, healing, architecture and art. But also at times we have been used to bring forward prophecy, guidance, of what was to occur, in order to forewarn and prepare. We were used as harbingers to pave the way for important events and individuals who would come to change the destiny of mankind. One such time of course was the birth of Jesus and I was chosen as the Angel of birth to bring this message to Mary, not as commandment but as question, to see if she would be willing to allow herself to be used as a vessel through which this birth would be made manifest. I was instructed to make it very clear to Mary as to what would be expected of her, of the judgements that would be made by others and her husband of her and her situation, of the pain and anguish, of the agony and sorrow that she would experience, as well as of the joys and wonder.

Such visions of the future, the great and grand predictions of her child, though startling and inspiring, were nothing more than dreams. Mary was a wise woman who even at such a tender age had been taught of the mysteries of the Divine Mother and knew that predictions uttered, even by an Angel, were not guaranteed to be truth, so powerful is the free will of mankind. And so of course her immediate thoughts turned to herself and the part that she would play – not only the indignation that she must endure but also the art and craft that she must exercise in raising such a powerful child and equipping it to cope with its destiny. Mary was a brave woman who assumed this duty and responsibility unfalteringly, who in the fullness of knowledge allowed herself to become the sacred vessel through which this great and powerful light would re-emerge upon the Earth and move forwards to carry the great and powerful energy of the Christ light into the world. With all this knowledge of what would be, she accepted this proposal, this invitation, and opened herself to receive a child of light.

Such events that occur in time, that mark the beginning of a change for the whole of mankind, that occur both physically and energetically in all planes, create echoes and ripples that vibrate backwards and forwards in time. Although it may be that December 25th is not an accurate calendar anniversary of the birth of Jesus, nevertheless because of mankind's conscious thought centring upon this occurrence at this time, they open themselves to the echoes of this great occurrence. Of course to some this is no more than a story, a fable and a fairytale represented by pretty images on Christmas cards and nothing more. But still these people to some extent will feel the rippling echoes of this powerful moment and be lit by the hope and light that it represented and represents now. For the past is not over, all moments of time in their own place being constant, and as such the light that rippled out from this moment still has power in the now which can be drawn upon, welcomed in, utilised and used to inspire and uplift, to create hope and joy, so that mankind may recognise that they are not alone but accompanied constantly by the presence of the Divine.

Some people say that there is no relevance now to the birth of this Master, of this messiah, that in this modern age where the global community has become so small and intelligent man and woman recognises that no one religion has dominance over the world, that we live in a multicultural society full of various religions, in this day and age where we must not allow ourselves to be dominated by a single truth, we should not put emphasis upon such a religious occurrence but rather focus on the underlying principles that are venerated at this time. Although this is true, it is also true that the essence of the mysteries and teachings, of the power and presence, of the significance of the birth of this child, is not Christian but something which transcends it, something which is found at the heart and core of every religion and something which every person at this moment in time can seize upon in order to make their life a better and brighter experience.

The birth of Jesus represented hope and was the fulfilment of a pattern that began a long, long time ago – the birth of hope in times of darkness, the emergence of light in the depth of night, the birth of the promised child in the depth of winter. A light that reminds us that we are not alone, that there is always hope and guidance and love that comes from the Source, the Creator of all, the Divine. A light that offers illumination and teaching, enlightenment and truth through its example and its words, through the nature of its being and the echo of its memory, through its burning presence and its desire to follow the path that was laid before it by the Divine. The echoes of such energy can be opened up to and welcomed in each time we gaze upon the image of a nativity, each time we sing a Christmas hymn. Each time our thoughts focus upon the essence of this Christmas story we can fill ourselves with the light of the Master Jesus and the Christ force, of the holy family and the sacrifices that they made for the whole world in order to bring forward the essence and epitome of the light, teaching and love of God the Divine Source.

The pattern that this singular and very famous occurrence echoes is seen in a number of different religions, including the religion which is native to the British Isles, the old pagan religion, the religion of the old ways. For at this time of the year the Goddess, the central figure within this religion, gives birth to a child of promise – to two children in fact, who represent in turn herself and her husband who has sacrificed himself in order to give life to the land. These children of promise grow and become the reincarnations of their parents – the child of light, the son, growing to become the oak king and the daughter growing to become the goddess of spring and summer. This constant cycle of the birth of light and life helps renew within us a sense of flow and grace and trust and belief that light will always, eternally follow darkness and lead us from the shadows into truth. And so, pertinent as the ever-moving cycle of the seasons, this story in its own way echoes the story of the birth of Jesus. Both are mysteries and patterns and in core the same; one occurring on the physical plane and the other a transcendent octave which has always been in the higher spiritual worlds. And so it goes on around the world and indeed there are places, other religions and cultures which in their own way celebrate the birth of light in times of darkness, acknowledge the presence and the power of the Divine when the world is in need.

It is important then at yuletide, at Christmas, to open yourselves to receive the echo of this love and also to utilise this moment to draw closer to us, the angelic kingdom. For when mankind's consciousness focuses on the existence of such beings, doorways and portals are opened whereby we Angels have greater access to the world and to mankind than ever before. And suddenly our presence can be known and seen, our light and life and laughter known. And we can move amongst men and women as we did; be seen, be experienced in a whole and total way. As you gaze upon each Christmas card, sing songs of Angels, focus on my part within the Christmas mystery, open yourself to the reality of our being and as such reaffirm to yourself that you are not alone.

And so my message for you this Christmastime, whenever you read these words, is this: I am the Angel of birth and have been present at the birth of all of mankind in all of their incarnations. As such too I am present at the death of all life, for death is a rebirth too and as I am midwife to life I am also midwife to afterlife. My message today is not about earthly death but it is about the death and rebirth of the soul that occurs as we journey through life and strive constantly to understand and make sense of our existence, journeying inwards and outwards in order to comprehend the nature of our evolution, of the part that we have to play, striving to grow, striving to expand, striving to be more than we are. This birth, this death, the death of ignorance, the birth of revelation, is a constant process of which I am aware and part of. And so today it is this that I speak of, this message that I give.

Christmas time, which lies towards the end of your year, is a dark time of light and can be for some a dark time of heart. Exhausted from the efforts that you have made throughout the year that has passed, it is common to find this time stressful and hard. And yet this is no more than the labour pains of rebirth, for the new year always brings to the hearts of many hope, a blank page extending before you in which anything may be written to atone and redeem yourself for those things that you have done that make you feel unworthy of the light and life and the true teachings that you wield and also infinite opportunities and possibilities to grow and to exercise your powers with greater restraint, subtlety, gentleness and light.

Pass through this dark time but as you do, feel the star rise in your heart, the light of Jesus being born. Know that this is the continuation of something which occurred before and which has always occurred in many different ways and forms and that you are part of this chain, this link. That each Christmastime as you open your heart to the returning of the light, you are reborn also – as saviour and messiah of yourself and the microcosm that is your world. Acknowledge that you are part of this Christmas miracle and each year decide how much you will surrender yourself to the birth of light that transpires inside you with all your knowledge of the difficulties as well as the loves that this will bring.

As I once delivered this message to Mary, so now do I deliver it to you. As you stand on the threshold of a new year it is your choice. Will you open yourself and be reborn in light to go forwards in full awareness to bring forward the true essential nature of your divinity? And if so how much will you do this? Trusting and then acknowledging that there is darkness to be experienced as much as there is joy. In order to make your decision it is important that you know the simple truth that I gave Mary that enabled her to find the courage and the strength to do what she did. You are not alone, never have been and never will be, but are always surrounded by the loving presence of the Divine and as such the Divine asks no more of you than you are capable of doing, and can be called upon, leaned upon and relied upon to provide you with the aid and assistance that you might need in enduring your path and finding within it the light of love and transformation.

Today we have spoken of ancient and mysterious things which may seem simple. The simplicity is an indication of their divinity and not to be underestimated but rather seen as a sign of the deep nature of their truth. Take all that has been said here and use it wisely and well to grow in light.

✦ ARCHANGEL ✦ MELCHIZADEK

The Angel of Communion

I am Melchizadek, the Womb of God, Archangel of Communion, bridge that spans the divide between the Divine that lives within limitless space and time and the limited universe that you call home. I was created before all other Angels that exist within your universe, born from the grace and splendour of the Divine to be the doorway, the portal through which the angelic continuum would be created, the angelic realm that exists this side of the veil. Angels were created before me in limitlessness, in divine time: the Cherubim and Seraphim, the Elohim, Metatron, the voice of God, but I was the first Angel to be forged whose toes would dangle in limited space, who would breathe breath into a universe filled with the mechanical movement of time, who would know reality as it is now. Even Lucifer, the Angel of Light, was born through me and all those who followed him. Michael and Raphael, Uriel and Gabriel, Azrael, all those Angels who form the continuum of light and life, who guard the elements of existence, who monitor over the energies and movements of reality, of the dimensions that co-join to create the universe in which you reside.

Mankind sees Angels in the light of their own consciousness. We have become stereotyped by mankind's assumption that we are specific to the Christian religion. In truth, of course, as extensions of the limitless Divine Source we are not connected or constricted to any one religion as seen or expressed or understood by mankind and have known many names and many faces throughout the history of mankind's religious exploration and tendency. But at this moment in time we are understood to be beings, winged and haloed, humanoid in form and shape and character. In essence, of course, we are none of these things. We are consciousness, energy, light, the perfect, constantly-changing, geometric, energetic shape and form of divinity in its purest and clearest nature. I am not a man, I am not a priest bedecked with wings, shining with a halo or aura of light. I am an intelligence, a conscious energy that bridges space and time and reality. I am a force through which the light of the Divine is made manifest through the angelic continuum here in this universal reality. I am a portal, a window, an opening, a bridge. I am Melchizadek, the Angel of Communion.

From time to time I have projected my energy, my consciousness, my intelligence, the nature of my essence, into Earth in order that I might communicate with mankind as to those things that are my speciality and the essence of my being. In accordance with Divine request I have touched the minds and hearts of men so that I might illuminate within them the importance of spiritual communion for their continued evolution and spiritual progression and in these times I have clothed myself in accordance with the consciousness of man's expectation and of late that has been as a man, many winged, surrounded with light, bearing symbols which enable the consciousness of those that might perceive me to understand in essence the nature of my being. My symbols are the rainbow, the bridge that spans the divide and also indicative of the nature of my prismatic function, to bring the light of God into the diversity of the angelic continuum, also the chalice and the bread, the tools of physical communion, representative of my function as

Angel of Communion not only to mankind but also to my brother and sister Angels, passing on to them the manna of the celestial heavens, the light and power of God so that they might utilise it in order to bring God's miracles to Earth. I am the distributor of this grace and these symbols then are fitting to both the angelic continuum that feeds through the nature of my window and because of the knowledge and power that through my grace God offers mankind too.

Communion is one of the great mysteries, one of the great secrets, one of the great truths. As with all of the great mysteries and truths, at one point in your history it was plain knowledge that all knew to be their universal and spiritual legacy. It was only as mankind evolved and developed that they began to segregate knowledge, keeping it, guarding it jealously from the masses and then these universal legacies became mysteries, became secret, sacred truths which were only ever half-shared with the masses, with the people. The mystery of communion is simple and yet profound. Communion is an opportunity whereby mankind might remind themselves of their intimate connection with the Divine Source, God. Where mankind might enter into a state of alignment with the Divine, where mankind might encourage their consciousness to expand and open like a flower to receive the light, intelligence, guidance, love and nurturing wisdom of the Divine which they are part of so that they might in time remember how to remain in this constant state of unity from whence they have come.

Separation, individuality, isolation, that that is the plague of mankind, the bane of mankind's existence, is an illusion. It is forgetfulness. It is an inability for mankind to believe themselves to be worthy of the truth that they are divine, that they are at one with the Source. It sounds simple, remembering is easy, entering back into this consciousness once the knowledge is given should be child's play and yet mankind has endured century upon century of conditioning that has led them to believe that they are not worthy, that they are not divine, that they cannot be in communion and connection with this great and infinitely pure source, that they are sinful and wrong, that they are evil and poor, that they are dark reflections of their perfect origin. These misconceptions have been bred by man who sought to control the masses by creating a religion, by distancing mankind from God and stealing from them their legacy and power. The truth has always remained but it now is hidden, suppressed by hundreds upon thousands of years of misinformation and misconduct which is why now, in the New Age, in the twenty-first century, in the time of Aquarius, mankind must be liberated to the truth and recognise the vital importance of communion.

As the portal that leads to the light of the Divine I have, in ages long since past, represented many things to many people, the essence and nature of Spirit itself in the earlier dynasties of Atlantis where I communicated to my priests and priestesses the secrets of my nature and my truth. I, like all angelic beings, am in essence elemental in nature which means that I am a consciousness that represents a profound reality, the reality of communion and spiritual existence. My nature is my mysteries and these were transmitted to the priests and priestesses of Melchizadek who were instructed to detach themselves from the royal family of Spirit, to whom I was originally patron, after that patronage was taken over by the Archangel Azrael and I released to other functions and duties. The priesthood of Melchizadek then endured, sustaining my mysteries and propounding them within the continent of Atlantis. They were guided by me to survive the great destruction, safeguard the truths that I had given them, the rituals, the knowledge and the hallows, some of which were dark, created by the Atlanteans then to reek unimaginable destruction upon the world, the priests and priestesses of Melchizadek being entrusted with the care of such dark artefacts, for it was known that they, and they alone, had light enough in order to shield the world from these things that could not be destroyed but only contained.

Encumbered then with this inheritance and with the knowledge and mystery of my craft and truth they endured, changing shape and form as the years rolled on, becoming the Order of the Violet Robe and then the Knights Templar. They altered and shifted their nature and way, allowing people to believe that they had been created by them when in truth they had always existed, but using their guiles, their mysterious powers, their magickal crafts, blended in to the worlds around them. The church who sponsored the Knights Templar knew of their ancient inheritance, adopted them, took in these orphans in the world and made them part of their own, knowing the powers and mysteries that they possessed and the damage that they could do if they unleashed these truths upon the world, sponsoring them, giving them a home, protecting them. The Knights Templar knew that the mysteries of the Divine were not yet to be revealed to the world and therefore were content to be shielded by those people who propounded the very illusions that they themselves carried the solution to. They were content to benefit from this protection and keep a watchful eye upon those that they knew in time they would have to rail against in order to bring the truth back to the world. But the church had other notions in mind. It adopted the Knights Templar and used them with one final intention always in mind: to destroy them and hide the mysteries of their truth forever. Although the Knights Templar were in

their classical form destroyed, their mysteries were pre-
served, they were transmitted, they were safeguarded, they
were hidden and the Knights Templar still exist to this day
in a different form.

The knowledge of Melchizadek endures and is spoken not
only here within these pages but by other channels and
prophets too and other teachers who have brought forward
many of the mysteries that are held beneath my wings: the
knowledge of sacred numerology and mathematics and its
appropriateness as the universal language, the power of
sacred geometry and its closeness to the nature of the
Divine and how these two things combined can be used to
free mankind from the artificial limitations of the calendar
that they have adopted, liberating them back to the cosmic
clock and freeing them to the greater spiritual legacy of
their own divine inherent power. Yes, there are others who
talk of these mysteries and more, who talk of the fabric and
structure, the very nature of the universe in which we live:
the flower of life and the Merkabah, the light vehicle, that
exists in embryo within the auric field and subtle bodies of
all men and women, which can be activated as a chariot of
light to carry them back towards the Divine through the
progression of consciousness and the development of
enlightenment, through the downloading of the Adam and
Eve Kadman into the energy system, correcting the imbalanced blueprints of their own nature. Yes, these mysteries are
spoken of but they are not to be spoken of here today. The
mystery that I have come forward to speak of is the one
which I began with, the mystery of communion.

At this moment in time, although the world experiences a
reawakening of spiritual truth there are still many who are
lost, who cannot find their way back to the Divine or to the
truth that they themselves are in essence divine inside.

Communion is the way. To align ourselves with God, to strengthen the axiatonal lines, the universal meridians that bind us to the weave, the web, the tapestry of life and through it back to the divine origin, the source of all light, to draw upon the manna of heaven, God's nurturing, loving hand through this intimate connection, by opening our hearts and allowing within us the spark of the Christ fire to be illuminated into a flame that will lead us back to our souls and through our souls and the grace of The Maitreya to the Divine Source, God.

Communion taken through the symbols of wine and bread, of flesh and blood, taken through the Christian magick of transubstantiation, is not essential. Communion occurs whenever someone prays, whenever someone turns their attention towards the Divine in any form of devotion, whether this is the singing of a hymn or the recitation of a Sanskrit mantra. Communion is not unique or individual only to Christian worship but is found to be part of every religion in varying different shapes and forms. Communion is partaking of the essence of the Divine, it is merging our consciousness with God's consciousness, it is opening our heart and mind so that we might be filled as a vessel with the light of our source and by so doing, and here is the important thing, being reminded that we are in essence ourselves divine. Communion acts through the law of resonance; we vibrate in commonality with the Divine because we are in essence and in embryo divine ourselves, have been born from divinity, and carry within us on a microcosmic level within the nucleus of our being, God. When the divine chord is played, when the divine light pours forth through the act of communion, whatever that act may be, the chord of divinity inside ourselves resonates with this present force and the two notes become one. We are aligned and attuned to our source and as such we are filled, we are strengthened, we are healed, we are aligned, we are connected to our spiritual path, to our higher self, to our guides and Guardian Angel, to the Divine Source, to the reason why we are and why we are here and we are reminded of the truth of our own nature.

Entering into a state of communion is not difficult though of course, as with all things, there are many different levels of communion that exist. The communion of body, the communion of mind, the communion of heart, the communion of spirit and soul and these depend upon the attitude with which we enter into communion and at times also the nature of the communion method that we use. However, whenever we enter into any type of communion we are strengthened and filled but maintaining that connection is the difficult thing. Maintaining a state of unity with the Divine is at best for most people upon the Earth at this moment in time a fleeting thing but in time through continued spiritual practice, through daily devotion, mankind can steer the nature of their consciousness and soul so that they can maintain at first a loose connection which in time grows stronger every day, to the Divine, so that they may be in full and open resonance with their source and in a constant state of communion and at oneness. This state, this mode of being is known as "unity consciousness", "enlightenment", "nirvana", "bliss", it is part of the process of ascension that leads to complete transformation of our identity, a reverting to our essential self.

My message here today is not to aim for enlightenment, for that is several steps away and there are other elements that need to be achieved besides communion in order for enlightenment or ascension to be brought into being; the absolution of karma, for instance, and also the completion of the reason for our being here. No, my message here today is to bring forward a simple means of communion that you may enter into daily in order to remind yourself of your divinity and shake off the limitation of your self-perception as "lowly human". This ritual then, this simple practice, is what I have come to give.

RITUAL

Clear a space for communion, clear some time. Use a space which is calm and still, a meditation area or a space within your home that you know will not be disturbed and which provides you with a sense of calmness, whether this is a bed-room or a living room or even the kitchen does not matter. You will need the traditional symbols of communion: a glass or chalice filled with wine, water or fruit juice and a small token of bread or a biscuit, something which can be eaten, something which can be broken. You may add to this other symbols, symbols that represent the rainbow, an image, a picture or a crystal that carries a rainbow inside it or a pic-ture of my likeness. You may if you choose also light a can-dle of deep magenta or rainbow colours to represent my presence and my energy. You may burn incense of a high vibrational nature such as frankincense or play in the dis-tance soothing music, though these are not particularly required. Seat yourself before the small collection of objects that you have created. Calm yourself, breathe slowly and deeply. Say this short prayer to call my attention and pres-ence into your space:

"Lord Melchizadek, Archangel of Communion, great source of light and love and truth, womb of God, bridge to the Divine, Master of mysteries of the spiritual realm, I call upon your presence and your power, enter into me, enter into my space, hold open the divide that exists in my consciousness and heart between myself and God and let the love of the Divine flow so that I may be reminded of my own divinity and through this unity be one and through this oneness grow. I open now like a flower to receive God's light through your grace."

Hold your arms away from your body, palms uppermost and tilt your head slightly backwards as if you were staring at the ceiling, close your eyes. Visualise the chakras of your body opening like flowers to receive the light of summer and visualise high above your head a great opening within the ethers and a tremendous down-pouring of brilliant white light. The white light passes into you and into the offering of your bread and wine. It flows into your chakras, through the meridians of your body and into the subtle forms of your aura, filling you with light until you are ablaze with the radiance of the Divine. There is a point where you and this light will become one. Where you are no longer receiving the light that pours down to you from heaven but where you and the light have merged completely as one essence, where you are the light, where you are the Divine and me, where there is nothing but oneness. Stay within this space for a moment; let the light of the Divine filter through your mind and heart, burning away your fears and problems, your worries, your aches and pains and woes, illuminating your thoughts, inspiring you, connecting you to the synchronicities of your life. Ironing out the wrinkles in your life path, aligning you to where you need to be, to what you need to do, to why you have come. Then after a while of staying within this space, see the light recede but know that you contain it now within you and blaze etherically like the sun. At this point you may drink a little of the wine and eat a little of the biscuit or the bread, leaving some to cast upon the earth as offering to the Divine Source, God. Know that the imbibing of the wine or water or juice and the eating of the biscuit or the bread are physical symbols only of what

already has occurred within and that they serve to strength-
en the grounding of the presence of the Divine within you.

END OF RITUAL

This small ritual can be done anywhere and within a short
space of time. It is best used when you are feeling low or
lost, disconnected from the Divine or from your path or
from the synchronicities of your life, though it can become
a regular spiritual practice performed every day if you so
desire. It will, as well as aligning you to the Divine Presence,
align you to me and to my mysteries and to my truths and
to my love. This power can be called also into foods or flowers that you might pass on to others who are less spiritually
or religiously inclined but who are in need of the presence
of the Divine within their life. The higher self is always open
to receive this communion and as the individual eats the
food or enjoys the flowers in their space, the light of God,
the light of communion will shine forth into their lives and
help to heal them.

Attending any form of communion ritual will also be very
powerful, particularly when you hold in your mind the relevance of that that you experience and acknowledge the
presence and power of my being within the space.
Remembering the small prayer that I have given will also
help open you to the communion experience more powerfully, however you might experience it. Know that communion is one of the essential practices that will lead you
towards spiritual growth and fulfilment and aid you in the
continuation of your path and is not to be underestimated
as a miraculous legacy and power.

My words here are almost spent and done but my mysteries
will continue to be unfolded within the minds and hearts of

men who remember me and my essence. Go forward then and know one thing above all others. You are the Divine and the Divine loves you and therefore as divine it is essential that you love yourself. In perfect love and perfect trust and faith I impart to you my blessings.

ARCHANGEL SANDALPHON

The Angel of Prayer

I am Sandalphon, twin to Metatron, Angel of Prayer and Angel of this sphere, the physical reality, and all that exists within it. The guidance that has come from my brother has unfolded the mysteries and truths regarding the nature of prayer and therefore my words here are not to replicate the importance of this holy act but rather to focus upon those other things that I am Angel of, rather to talk about my dominion over this reality and explain in more detail how the nature of my duties and responsibilities differ from those of that more famous Angel of the earth element, the Archangel Uriel. The Archangel Uriel is the Angel of the earth element, one of those sacred seven elements that make up the universe in which you humans live. He presides not only over the Earth as a planet itself but more specifically over the element of earth which is part of your planet's makeup.

I, however, am the Angel of this sphere, not only of your world but of that space, that dimension in which your physical world is located and all those contributory dimensions below the physical plane and above it that fall within the first sphere of the seven spheres that reach upwards towards the Divine. The seven spheres are collections of interacting dimensional realities, interpenetrating frequencies which are levels of consciousness and dimensional spaces all at once, simultaneously, both combined. I am here to speak of the first sphere and all the various interacting energies located within this segment of dimensional space and reality.

There are dimensions below the world in which you live. The dimension of lost spirits and the limbo dimension where those who take their own life and those who die suddenly, who hold deep and dark negative thoughts about themselves sometimes, fall to and there are dimensions which interpenetrate your reality on a higher frequency: the pranic planes and the astral plane, for instance. But first let me speak of this dimension, the physical reality in which you find yourself now.

Your physical reality is a mirror of your nature. It is the macrocosmic reflection of your microcosmic being and you and it are symbiotically connected and at one. Without you the Earth could not be nor the universe that holds it; and without them, the universe and this world, you could not exist. You are part of the same pattern, the same design, the same fabric, the same weave, part of the same canvas and therefore dependent upon each other for your existence and being. What you do to yourselves, as a race, reflects upon the macrocosm of your world and the universe that holds it and although this cannot be greatly seen at this moment in time, it is beginning to reveal itself as so in the way in which your world now suffers because of the way in which you, mankind, have neglected your holistic health and nature.

Your scientists have already discovered that your world is symbiotically connected. That despite the space that separates one piece of its geographical location from another there are connections that result in the Earth responding as a whole to situations that occur in particular areas throughout your globe. Your scientists also have discovered and believe that the degradation of the protective layer of the ozone in your world has come about as a direct result of the pollution that you have, initially unwittingly, unleashed upon your world in times now past, and although this is in part true the degradation of your world, the global warming that you experience, the rapid changes to climate, the alteration and disharmony of the seasons and the changes and transformations that are occurring in the poles of your planet, are a manifestation of the unruly behaviour of your psyche and your hearts upon each other and upon yourself and the disarray that has been created due to your own neglect.

In ancient times, now long since lost to legend, myth and fantasy, those people who worshipped the old ways of the Earth and the Divine acknowledged the interconnection between themselves and the world in which they lived. They knew and recognised that they had a responsibility in turning the wheel of the seasons and maintaining the health and balance of their planet through their own actions towards themselves and towards the planet around them. Kings in ancient times knew when they married their queen that she was a symbolic representative of the Gaia Spirit, the Goddess of the Earth, and through the king's honouring of her, he honoured the land and ensured its balance and its safety. And if, for whatever reason, this honouring was brought into disarray, he would at times be called upon to sacrifice himself to the land in order to appease the offence that he had caused the great Goddess in this way. This truth, however, has long since been confined to old wives' tales and mythology but there is truth within it. Every woman through her femininity is connected to the Earth and the presence of the Gaia Spirit, the Goddess, as every man through his sexuality is connected to the masculine polarised presence of the Divine found in nature, the Green Man god, Herne, Cernunnos, the presence of the solar intelligence of the Divine. And so although I have come to speak of the full array of your dimension, it is on this subject that I have come to impart my most important message. For it is very important at this time, when your world hangs in a very delicate and precarious balance, that you must try to redress the mistakes that your forefathers have made and acknowledge the intimate connection that exists between you and your physical reality and by beginning to be more mindful and attentive to your own internal balance of mind, body and spirit bring about directly into your location a greater balance within the Earth itself.

If one man or woman within their town or village attempted to be more self aware, more spiritual in the finest meaning of the word, more mindful of their thoughts and feelings, of their physical well-being, of their spiritual progression and evolution, they would beneficially affect their location and surrounding to such a powerful and positive extent that it would contribute greatly to outweighing all those others who did not comprehend or acknowledge the interconnection that existed between themselves and their world. Such is the power of the spiritual intent amongst the ignorant and blind. This is how it has always been and this is why there is still hope. If one person in a city or town acknowledged the equinoxes, sabbats and solstices, contributed in their own simple way to turning the wheel and resurrecting the balance of the seasonal shifts, they would contribute greatly to amending that that has been lost and damaged by all those other people's ignorance concerning the importance and need of these simple and beautiful acts of honouring and consecration. If but a small percentage of people in regard to the total population of your planet honoured the ancient, simple, beautiful and magickal ways, acknowledging the intimate, powerful connection that exists between themselves and the manner of the living of their life and the world around them, your world could not

only be saved but also be transformed. And the transformation of your world, of course, is imperative in regard not
only to the evolution of those people who dwell upon it but
also the evolution of the spirit of your world itself and the
evolution that is to take place within your universe, the
Earth being pivotal within this transformation. And this
transformation not only incorporates the honouring of the
Earth and the redressing of the imbalance that has been created throughout the generations that have passed but also
the clearing and cleansing of those levels of reality where
the spirits of the dead have become Earthbound and
trapped in the limbo dimensions.

Earthbound spirits, those who do not know that they are
dead or refuse to enter the light, for whatever reason, or
those who are too traumatised by the process of their passing to successfully move into the next world, inhabit largely the same dimension in which you rest, separated only by
a very small vibrational frequency and of course a lack of
physical form. But those who look upon themselves darkly,
for whatever reason, and who consider themselves to be sinful
and beyond salvation or unworthy of entering into heaven or
the spiritual world, have plummeted into a dimension
which rests below yours known as "limbo" or "purgatory"
or "hell". This dimension has not been created as a form of
punishment by the Divine Source but is a space where
people who judge themselves harshly in this manner fall to
naturally, because of the nature of the deepening of their
vibrational status, and in this realm, which is largely created
by the intent and will of those who journey to it, find that
they arrive in a hell or purgatory which is directly reflective
of the nature of their own recrimination. They find themselves in a dark, loathsome place and are often completely
unaware of the other presences that reside there, concerned
and consumed only by the wrongdoings of their own

nature. Therefore, often in this space those who have taken their own life find that they awaken to this hell. All those who have lived their lives in regret and shame and guilt, all those who through the illusions of a condemning religion believe themselves to be beyond redemption, find that they have awoken to a hell that has been predicted and pro-grammed for them by those who in truth know nothing of the Divine but everything of the politics of mankind.

As much as the Earthbound who share your world with you need to be rescued and carried into the spiritual world, into the light, so too do those who have plummeted into limbo. Many mediums who have the capacity to perform such res-cues are fearful of entering into such works because there is an element of danger involved but largely because there are even more risks of experiencing great sadness, darkness, deso-lation and pain. Many mediums are reluctant to willingly throw themselves into such negativity and so choose finer and lighter pursuits to employ their gifts upon. And so more and more throughout the years, as people have turned away from this very important vocation, the limbo realms have become more and more full of the souls that have self-damned themselves. Now more than ever then work must be done to liberate these poor lost, anguished beings and also to clear from your dimension the lost souls who roam it seeking the light. The rescuing of these beings is also undertaken by Angels and spiritual guides and by the animal kingdom, which employs various members of its own king-dom to go into the darker dimensions of limbo to create compassion within the hearts of the hopeless, so that they might once again remember what it is to love and through this mercy and compassion set themselves free, the animal kingdom knowing that the despair that they encounter there is only illusionary and therefore not being infected by it themselves. In this way the animal kingdom is far wiser than the kingdom of living man who is so fearful of an illusion that they are all too aware of.

The liberation of these souls, however, can be undertaken by man, even those who are not particularly mediumistically inclined, by regularly praying for the liberation of these beings and anchoring and earthing the light of the Divine into this kingdom and the lower realms, by praying in groups or alone, by calling upon the light divine and those high angelic presences who work in this way, enabling the high angelic forces of the Archangels Michael and Azrael, of the Archangels Gabriel and Raphael, to utilise their physical vessels and their lower energy to enter into these darker spaces, channelling this angelic light into these low dimensions so that it may more efficiently liberate those lost there. Humans can gather together, the sooner the better, and pray for those areas where disasters have occurred, where great acts of horror have taken place, where people are guaranteed to have become lost after death, ensuring that the lost spirits are more efficiently guided into the light and not left to roam and become confused after their death. Humans through simple prayer can ground the light of the higher celestial heavens and enable Angels to reach further into the deeper darkness within your sphere, liberating the lost and guiding them home.

Those who possess mediumistic talents and the ability to travel out of form can, by calling upon the aiding presence of their guides and Guardian Angels, descend themselves into these spheres to liberate the lost and lonely through counselling and love, by shining the light of their compassion into these places and acknowledging that whatever they may encounter there is purely an illusionary creation generated by those who do not consider themselves to be worthy of salvation. They can, with all confidence, enter into these places unharmed and set these people free. And these are people, each and every one of them, lost spirits, no different from you other than that they no longer possess a body and have become homeless because of their despair, because in life they did not comprehend the simple truth, that truth being that the Divine Source loves them irrespect-ive of who and what they are and what they might have done, that they are not judged by the Divine but only by themselves and therefore all are welcome into the higher realms of heaven.

As for those other dimensions which interpenetrate your sphere, there are those places where the fragments of your traumatised spirit journey to when you experience shock and pain, those dimensions that shamans, wise men and witches, ancient women of their tribes have always jour-neyed to, to rescue the splintered parts of your spiritual essence. But it is not my part here to go into more detail regarding the nature of this dimension today. It is important only for you to know of its existence so that you may, if you so choose, discover more about it in regard to your own well-being and the well-being of others.

There are also those higher dimensions which interpene-trate your own such as the pranic kingdoms where the uni-versal life force, the radiance of the Divine Intelligence, can be accessed in order to provide you with life and energy, as much as water and food do, the lower pranic realm being that emanation of the Divine that feeds your physical form and etheric body, the root, sacral and solar plexus centres within your energy system and the realm of higher prana being the emanation of the Divine, the universal life force, chi, that feeds the heart, throat, brow and crown, your emo-tional and mental faculties.

All that you need to understand in regard to these dimensions is that at this moment in time in towns and cities, the prana that you ingest is poor. When we breathe prana into our being we release into the atmosphere anti-prana which is the antithesis of life-enhancing prana. The waste components of the prana that we ourselves digest, anti-prana, is transformed back into positive prana by the sea and by the wildlife of your world, in much the same way that carbon dioxide is recycled and transformed back into oxygen. But in cities, where there is no sea, no natural flowing water and no trees or little vegetation to transform the anti-prana back into positive prana, the atmosphere becomes clogged and polluted by negative polarised pranic energy which when ingested again contributes to the clogging of the energetic system and the depletion of an individual's immunity and energy. After a time, this energy is replenished, usually by the changing weather conditions which move the anti-prana into different parts of your world where it can be more easily transformed. This is why it is vitally important for all those of you who reside within towns and cities that you find greater access to the countryside, to the sea, on regular occasions so that you may ingest positive forms of prana more efficiently and therefore restore yourselves for your continued living within these cities and towns where it is difficult to access the full glorious energy and the might of God.

Tai Chi, Chi Kung, Yoga, Pilates, ancient systems which focus upon the importance of breathing in prana and distributing it within the body, are the remnants of ancient truths passed from the beginning of time to mankind, from Angels, that would enable man to successfully balance the life force energy within their being. The relevancy of these practices now, more than ever before, is vital in order for mankind not only to live efficiently, effectively, healthily, balanced and well but also to have lives that provide you with a foundation for evolution and spiritual growth. Therefore, all of those who ardently seek to develop and grow spiritually should be regularly practising one of these disciplines in order to ensure the distribution and balance of universal life force, pranic energy, within the bodily system.

Your world is a complex and beautiful part of the universe. The laws of limitation that govern it prescribe certain dimensions which form it to play part of the process of your existence's unfoldment. It is vital and relevant for all those who seek to master themselves and the universe in which they live to gain a clearer understanding of these dimensional locations as described in theosophy through the sacred systems of the seven spheres and the Tree of Life, the Kabbala, the ancient Judaic system which explains the principal manifestations of the Divine from the highest realms of heaven to the lowest realms of the physical world in which you live.

In this discourse I have mentioned but a few of the different locations and spaces that co-exist within your reality, the astral plane being the last of these that I will talk about here. The astral plane is a sphere which contains within it many different components to do with the mental plane and also the plane in which elementals reside. It is important because it houses not only the place in which your thoughts take on form and eventually reality, a place which is used greatly in creative visualisation or magickal manifestation, but also because of that layer which houses the elemental beings and because of their interplay with your physical dimension and your home. It is important for you to understand through my discourse that the astral plane is part of your world. It exists because of your previous actions that have forced the elemental kingdom to reside in a dimension which did not always exist but which was created in order to house a race of ancient beings who were created by the Divine at the beginning of time to be the gardeners of your world and who were forced to abandon it by the narrow-mindedness of your world's religions who believed them to be manifestations of the devil, a presence which is wholly illusionary.

The time is coming where the Earth is changing, where new things are blossoming and blooming and where old truths are resurfacing. Some of the changes that will be made upon your world will take it back to a glorious state that it once inhabited and the return of the elemental kingdom is one of these transformations. It is vital that you, as a race, learn to reconnect with these presences and find once again their relevance and intimate connection not only to your world but also to you.

I am Sandalphon, I am the Angel of this sphere and it is my duty to govern it and protect it as best I can, to inform you of its multifarious nature and to encourage you to work with the laws and conditions that are in play here, to encourage you to understand the various different dimensions of consciousness and reality which are part of the physical universe. This ritual then is to honour the world in which you live and your connection with it. It is a simple ritual of balance and it is a ritual also of hope and evolution.

RITUAL

The ritual is a very short, succinct and sweet one. It is a ritual which can be performed once a week or once a month, alone or in a group. It is for personal alignment and balance and also to offer oneself as a conduit through which the light of the angelic kingdom may shine into your world in order to encourage the restoration of balance. It is a ritual particularly which can be done after disaster or trauma in any locational space within your planet itself.

Stand with your feet shoulder-width apart and raise your arms so that they are parallel with your shoulders, so that your body creates a five pointed star shape. Turn your palms uppermost and raise your head slightly as if you were look-ing towards the ceiling. Have someone read these words or memorise them beforehand and say them at this point, or record them and play them so that you may hear them:

"I open myself to the higher heavens and surrender myself as a vehicle and conduit through which the light of the Angels divine may shine. I ask that this light be cast forth into the world and into the dimensions that fall beneath it so that this light may play its part in redressing the imbalance that exists here and in offering a star of hope to those who have lost their lives and descended into confusion, roaming the Earth lost and lonely and afraid or descending deeper into the realms of limbo and purgatory. I ask that this light also be used to redress the imbalances caused by ignorance and pain, caused by foolishness and arrogance, caused by fear and greed and that the physical world be restored through my grace and my will and through the restoration of the balance of my spirit, my body, my mind, my heart and my soul I ask that all wounds be healed; I ask that the love of the Divine be centred here in me and radiate from me out into the world. This is my will and my desire; let it then be so. So mote it be. Amen."

See the light descend from heaven, falling like a curtain or a shower into the heart and radiating through the arms and feet, through the head, into the world around you; see it fly through the universal meridians, the axiatonal lines, the thread of your reality; see it descend into the darkest dimensions of limbo; see it reach out to the astral kingdoms and the elementals there, like a warm light inviting them closer; see the light flow through the subtle bodies of your aura, bringing about a symbiotic healing of Earth and human, of heart and world, of body, mind and soul and of the spirit of Gaia, the consciousness of your world. After a while let the radiance pass through you, resume a normal standing position and give your thanks to the realm of the Angels.

END OF RITUAL

Yours is a very special world, a very beautiful world, a world that was created with great delicacy and mindfulness. Remember the beauty contained within it and remember that as an integral part of it, as an integral part of its make-up, you are responsible for it and have the power to redress the damage that has been done through your intent and loving mindfulness of yourself and of the world itself too. Take this responsibility not as a burden but as a loving gift. In peace and truth I take my leave and leave you with my love.

ARCHANGEL
✦ RATZIEL ✦

The Angel of Hidden Things

My name is Ratziel and I am the Angel of Hidden Things, things veiled and unseen, things obscured and buried. I am the Angel of secrets, of truths that have been lost or mislaid. I am the Angel of the dark, of confusion, of obscurity and vagueness. I am the bringer of light and illumination, of realisation and truth. I am the lamp and the light and the eye that sees within it, I am the veil lifted, I am the mystery understood, I am the initiate and the initiation and I am those who rise from these challenges reborn.

The word "occult" has frightened many people because they do not understand the true nature of its meaning. "Occult" simply means "hidden", those things that are obscured. It is a word which represents the unseen world, the supernatural, the plane in which all things are lumped together that most men have no logical or rational explanation of; witchcraft and magick, mediumship and psychical ability, unfathomable phenomena and the majesty and miraculous nature of the Divine. All these things fall within my dominion, all these things I watch over and guard, guide people to and reveal. All these things are part of who and what I am.

From my lofty vantage point upon the Tree of Life I gaze down upon the world of men and upwards towards the worlds of the Divine. I am, of course, as every Angel is, an extension of the consciousness of the One but having been given life and form to monitor over those things that are shrouded in mystery I have a unique perception that enables me to see how people respond to those things within my care. How people are often frightened by those things that intrigue them so much that despite themselves they can do nothing other than pick at the very fabric that separates them from their own fears and insecurities. Mankind contains within them part of the curiosity of the Divine that led to the creation of this universe and world in which we all reside. It was the Divine Source's need to know more about itself that created limited space and time and encouraged the Divine to place itself within it, creating not only the angelic kingdom but also the kingdom of mankind. Mankind is a microcosm of the macrocosm of the One, the Divine Source, and as such contains within him all of the Divine's inclinations including curiosity and the need to know. It has been mankind's insatiable drive since the beginning of its existence to discover who and what and why it is and even though those answers, which have always lain in the dark just beyond the reach of mankind, have terrified them they have also fascinated them and driven them to outshine their fear and dare to enter into the darkness of uncertainty to find the truth.

It is then curiosity and daring that bring an individual to me. They shine like sparkling gems or stars within an aura of a person who begins to question and open their mind to possibilities and truths previously outside their consciousness or concern. They start to prod and pick away at the thread that binds the veil between themselves and the unknown world and it is then upon my dark wings that I swoop in to shed a little light through the seams that have been unpicked by the questioning fingers of the seeker. My light illuminates, enables the shadows to be cast away and the truth to be seen. It provides people with the knowledge that they need in order to know the truth that they have always hungered for.

Once an individual begins to seek, the path that they open before them is unstoppable. Knowledge once learnt cannot be forgotten. It changes an individual. Even if after some time they decide no longer to believe what they have chosen as their foundation, they will always be altered by that which they have entertained, and if that which they have entertained is truth, their denial of it will not leave them beyond redemption. An individual can use the power of their free will to deny a truth once they have seen it but the truth once seen changes and the changes that are made can never be undone. The individual may close their eyes and wall up their ears so that they may not be exposed to further truths but the truth inside them will rest there waiting for the right moment to continue to grow. Each individual carries inside them the power of discernment. This is truth that exists within their heart of hearts, within their divine core. It is what guides an individual to truth. This is a light, a pearl, a star, a guiding presence which is often suppressed but which from time to time is allowed to shine its light and lead its individual to a person or a place or a piece of information that will contribute to the liberation of their consciousness and spirit, to the evolution of their soul. When an individual is exposed to truth, the discerning light inside them recognises it and even if their conscious mind refutes the truth that they have seen, their shining spark will attach itself to this pearl of wisdom and not let it go. Although they may deny what they have seen or heard, deep down inside they will be changed and this is why it is essential, irrespective of the seeming result of the interaction or sharing of truth between one person and another, to continue to

expose the truth that all of you have found to others. You
are not seeking to convert. This is where mankind has made
mistakes since the beginning of time. No, what you are simply seeking to do is share the truth that you have found with
others and trust and know that this truth once exposed and
shown will play its part and make its mark within the hearts
and minds of men.

My power is to illuminate. I can be called upon to assist
each and every individual who seeks truth as well as to assist
those people who walk along the path of their lives blindly.
If the moment is not right I will not shine my light upon
them but if their soul agrees that they are in need of illumination, then called upon by petition or prayer, I will focus my
light upon all and any who are in truth in need of it.
Illumination can often come as a rude awakening to many.
When they have closed their eyes and ears so tightly, to be
suddenly stunned by the light of truth can be frightening
and traumatic but if this occurs then it occurs for a reason.
It occurs because that person needs at that moment in time
to be catalysed in such a way and although there is danger
in such alchemy, the risk is often one which the higher self
is willing to take. The higher self is content for certain lives
to be wasted. There are experiences that can be made and
contributions that can be given to the world around the
individual that do not require spiritual awakenment but
ultimately it is the soul's aim to release its karma, to contribute that that it has come to give to the Earth and to
evolve, and therefore after a while of persistent obtuseness
the higher self will risk the sanity of an incarnation in order
to expose it to light that may begin a quest for evolution,
exposed and open consciousness and divine truth.

The power of my light then is dangerous and this is something also which mankind has always been aware of subcon-

sciously and fearful of. That the occult world is not only a world full of ghosts and ghouls but light and truth which burn and dazzle and which once exposed to, change for ever the individual who peers inside the Pandora's box that is within my keeping. But the light that I carry is essential, it is an ingredient that is required for all to grow and therefore, although largely in the past my presence has been hidden and obscured, I have always been close by the side of those who have sought the truth. Consciousness moves up and down the scale of truth, as mankind has progressed through various periods of history, starting on a high, Lemuria and Atlantis, plummeting quickly but rising and falling from time to time as the civilisations of the world have risen and fallen. The falling state of consciousness is not a state which leads a civilisation to debauchery and perversion but rather materiality. It is a state of consciousness whereby an individual loses their way and distances himself from God by aligning himself to a world which is largely illusionary, a world of science and fact. Although science mirrors the spiritual world it is only that, a series of rules and explanations that make mankind feel more comfortable living within a world which is formed from mystery and magick. The lost consciousness of many has often been because of this and because of mankind's greed and need to provide themselves with false security by immersing themselves in a world full of material assurance. The primary lack of awareness that has driven mankind to bury themselves so much within the material world is their fear of death which of course is, in itself, an illusion. Death is a transformation, the move from one state of awareness to another. Nothing ever truly dies, science testifies to this. Things simply are changed, rearranged and reborn as something else. Life is eternal but mankind's unexpected ignorance at this truth has led them to seek solace in material security to provide them with a comfort and a confidence that will cosset them from their fear of oblivion. Mankind will learn in time that no amount of material security can cosset them from the changes and transformations that are bound to occur when they cross the threshold between life and death and are reborn and often it is death that stirs the first awakening within the conscious minds of many.

At this moment in time mankind's consciousness is beginning to rise and mankind is beginning to question the nature of their world, the whys and wherefores of their life. More than ever before I am busy attending to those seekers who awaken daily, trying to find their way in a world which is cluttered with false material truths. I am the mantra that is spoken and the meditation that is made, the prayer that is entered into and the ritual that is enacted. I am the knowledge within the book that people read. I am the lecture that is attended. I am the desire within the heart to be free and to know the truth. In ancient times, when the consciousness of man was dim, I was called upon to find hidden treasures, for I am the Angel who finds things, who reveals those things that have been lost. I was heartily misunderstood and those who dabbled in such powers for such petty reasons were often chided harshly for their attempts to call upon heavenly powers for such banal reasons. But now I am seen again as I am meant to be seen, as the Angel who offers light where there is darkness. And so the ritual that I bring is one that can be performed for you yourself or on behalf of others: those who seek light, those who seek truth, those who seek their way. It can be used when an individual first starts their journey or when an individual has become slowed upon their path, obscured or blocked by themselves or others or circumstances and situations. It is a ritual that can be called upon to help those who have become entangled and confused in ways that they once thought were the truth but which have revealed themselves to be nothing more than diversions. My power aligns and reveals. My power provides people with hope.

RITUAL

For this ritual you will need a few very simple things: a white candle in a candlestick which is unlit and veiled with a black square of silk or other material. In darkness sit before the unlit veiled candle. Call upon my name using this prayer or one similar to it:

"Ratziel, Angel of the occult, I call upon your presence and your power. Out of the darkness come, hear the words of this seeker and bring them aid, for I am lost in the darkness and seek light, for I need help in finding my way, for I have mislaid myself upon my path and need to rediscover the direction in which I must now turn. Angel of illumination, bring me light."

Take the veil from the candle and light the candle with a match. Let the illumination burn brightly into the darkness of your space. Stare at the burning candle flame for a moment and then close your eyes and let the light of my illumination shine like a ray into the areas of your life, into your mind and heart, into your being, into the worlds supernal[1] and spiritual around you, illuminating all. Be aware of which thoughts might enter into your mind: images, words, the titles of books, the images of faces. Let any and all guidance that comes enter into you.

If no guidance comes at this time then do not despair, I work

---

* On the Tree of Life there are two triangles formed by the Sephiroth. The one that points downward is called the supernal triangle and it refers to the higher consciousness of the Divine.

in many ways and will find a way of guiding you to the person and place and situation that you need in order to lift you from the darkness that you are in. Sometimes the illumination of my rays needs time to burn through the thick blanket of obscurity that has settled in your mind and it will be over a number of days that the dim light of illumination will burn through and the guidance will become clear.

After you have sat in front of the candle for a little while, offer this prayer of gratitude before you extinguish the candle's flame:

"Ratziel, Angel of the unseen world, I thank you for your assistance and your aid in this endeavour and bid you hail and farewell."

END OF RITUAL

My nature is not only to point people in the right direction but to provide people with answers and truths. I am an Angel of knowledge after all and part of the way in which I can unveil things is by providing people with information. I can be called upon then to wax lyrical about the metaphysics of the universe, to provide people with understanding regarding the mechanics of how things work or how things can be done. As an Angel of knowledge I can provide people with prophecies and truth, information taken from the Akashic records of a personal nature or of a more universal nature too and have throughout history in various guises provided various people with information that they have sought from the universe. Angels are invisible things, modest and humble in their nature. They do not require fame. They do not need to be mentioned. We speak through the whispers of the wind and inspire by touching the heart with our wings. Many people who have brought forward to the Earth great occult and spiritual truths have received these thunderbolts of lightening from me but have never known my name or face. Do not forget then to whom you can call when you seek understanding or further explanation of a spiritual truth that has left you dumbfounded. The invisible world is not intangible and impractical but can provide great and comprehensive understanding regarding many things.

The final thing then that I have come to speak of is another use that I might be called upon for, for as I am the unveiler so too am I the veiler of things. An Angel of dichotomy and duality am I, capable of hiding things and making things unseen. Often in times now long since past I was called upon to veil those sorcerers and priests who chose not to be seen by others, to make them invisible to the occult eye and sometimes to the human eye too. To veil their light so that darker forces would not seek them out. To make them like the shadows, part of the scenery, unnoticed, unheard. Of course, any who call upon this part of my power must do so for the right reason or they may incur karma or simply an un-obliging hand. But those who call upon me to protect them in this way, to veil and shadow them, will meet my good assistance so long as their intentions are good.

I can also be called upon to veil situations, situations that may create unwelcome attention, things that have been done which are arousing suspicion or gossip within a community, creating the beginnings of slander. I can quiet down interest in a situation by making it unseen and so when the evil impish amongst mankind and in the other world too seek to assail an individual by aiming the prejudice of mankind towards them, I am the Angel to call upon in order to lower their profile until such time as it is safe for that individual's light to be seen. My power works doubly here: to illuminate the minds of those suspicious so that they might more clearly understand the true nature of the individual's endeavours and not be fooled into thinking that they are practicing dark and malevolent acts. As a veiler of things my protection is not defensive or aggressive in nature but works as a distraction and because of its ways is powerful and easy to procure. It is worthwhile then to remember this in the future.

I am Ratziel. I am the Angel of the occult sphere, the Angel of hidden truths and secrets long forgotten. Many are the mysteries contained within my heart and mind. Many are the treasures of ancient texts and tomes that have long since fallen to dust on Earth held within my hands, within my lips. Call upon me in times of need and all of these mysteries and magicks may be yours. For now I take my leave and leave with you my love, Ratziel, your servant and guide.

ARCHANGEL
✦ CASSIEL ✦

The Angel of Contemplation

I am Cassiel of the Seventh Star, Angel of Contemplation, introspection and self-enquiry. I am the Angel known by other names who represents the force and power sometimes seen and acknowledged as Saturn, the bringer of karma, the unveiler of destiny, the hand of fate. I am known sometimes as Zaphkiel though in truth Zaphkiel and Cassiel are one. I am a power that is integral and essential for forward movement, spiritual evolution, ascension and growth, a power which is great and prevalent but often unseen and unknown. I am the mirror of silence that descends unbidden at odd and unpredicted times to confront the chattering mind with its own image. I am the deep stillness of meditation and prayer that enables that to be seen which is hidden, the true face of the spiritual seeker that has been veiled, suppressed, shadowed for far too long. Created by the Divine to assist mankind in finding their divinity, it is my power that steers people towards their own inner truth, a truth which is often uncomfortable to see and difficult to digest but which leads ultimately towards the one true revelation that all are one and that this one is the Divine.

The society in which you live at this moment in time is one which no longer teaches the value of contemplation or provides instruction as to how it is to be entered into. Moments therefore where my energy can descend have to be

snatched, stolen from situations which emerge in seemingly coincidental or unplanned ways to catch mankind off
guard, to use enforced periods of solitude and silence to
steer the consciousness inwards towards itself where conclusions can be found that can enable the consciousness, the
mind of man, to be set free. These moments occur in the
strangest of places and the oddest of times: on long journeys
where there is nothing to do other than think; in those
rooms within the home where we are protected from the
disturbances of our life, where we are not distracted by the
irrelevant mundanities of existence. Some, of course, seek
me out, place themselves in situations whereby they urge
themselves to contemplate and confront their hidden selves
and these beings are admirable and sometimes foolish in
their endeavour, for only those who are ready to gaze upon
their own face can extract from these opportunities positive
growth and, as is the same with gazing at the face of God,
if you are not ready to contemplate the true nature of your
being there is great risk that you can be damaged and
burned. My discourse here then is in part instruction and
understanding as to the nature, power and relevance of contemplation so that you may more fully understand it and
more confidently enter into it so that you may draw upon
my presence and my skill and use it wisely and well to grow.

Contemplation then is the facing of oneself. It is turning
our thoughts away from distraction and the world around us
in order to explore deeply our thoughts and thought
processes and our feelings and their origins and our motiv-
ations and our actions. It is contemplating the nature of the
foundation of our being: why we are here, what we are to
do, why we do the things that we do. It is contemplating
who we are in essence. Not our job or our position in society, not our social background or the classification of our
education but the true essence of our being, our essential

nature. It is an opportunity to recognise and release illusionary conditioning that has been created by our parents and
our society, by our educational systems and the false truths
that we have been fed by science and the physicists in the
world around us. It is an opportunity to recognise what we
truly believe and what we truly have experienced. To contemplate what we want to become. Why we are here and
how we can achieve it. To try to sense and feel the nature of
our soul purpose and path, to align to the divinity that exists
inside our own being.

The divinity within man, the true essential self, that part of
them that is their soul, their higher being, is like a tiny star
contained within the centre of their hearts. The heart chakra
is a window, an aperture that allows the light of the soul, the
higher self, to shine through. It shines through the construct
of the ego, the lower self, the personality self. This is in itself
a vehicle that enables us to experience reality and to contribute to it. A vehicle which is created, largely, by our initial experiences of life, by the contributory instructions of
our parents, by our culture, society, religion and teaching as
well as by the karmic inheritances that we bring forward
from our former lifetimes. The soul then shines through this
lens, through this vehicle and expresses itself, magnified,
warped, channelled and coloured in this way. As we aim
towards spiritual evolution, towards self-discovery and
recognition, we undoubtedly begin to chisel away at the
lower self, the spirit, recognising those parts of ourselves
which are in truth illusions which have been created via the
opinions and perceptions of other people about us which
are not true. And the more we chip away at these illusions
the more the light of the soul shines through, the more our
essential self becomes apparent. The essential self then is a
combination of the light of the soul and the light of our
spirit, which is not formed from illusion or the perspectives

of others but rather from our experiences of the reality around us. This combination of spirit and soul creates, symbolically, the hexagram, the co-joining of the higher and lower self to create the essential being.

This transformation is brought about largely by contemplation of who we are and why we are here and this is achieved undoubtedly in many different ways: in meditation, on mental, emotional or physical journeys that we take in life, instigated and prompted by tragedies and challenges and initiations but always nurtured by silence. Silence is a mirror you see. Silence is the smooth reflective surface of the lake that allows us to see ourselves. Any other noise is a distraction, however simple or beautiful it may be; it allows the consciousness to fix upon it and use it in order to create distortion and illusion of its own nature. Silence has nothing to offer other than the perfect reflective state that we need in order to more clearly and completely contemplate ourselves. Contemplation, however, is an art. It is not something which can be mastered quickly but something which we must gently enter into over time. If we imagine that our true self lies at the bottom of a lake which has become obscured and clouded over time by sediments that have fallen upon it, then we can see how contemplation (which is not unlike placing our hand into the lake and stirring the grime at the bottom of it up in order to find the true essential self which lurks below) then we can see how contemplation can initially create confusion and greater obscurity, as the sediment at the bottom of the lake is disturbed and floats to the surface, sullying and polluting the clearer part of the water that we have maybe strived to achieve for quite some time, making our initial experience of contemplation negative, disruptive and wholly unpleasant. In time, however, our fumbling in the dark enables more of the sediment to be removed. Piece by piece we filter away the grime that has been dislodged from the bottom of our lake and more and more small nuggets of the truth emerge. In time the sediment is cleared and the true essential self is found, a treasure hiding beneath the stillness. When we gaze into the lake then, we see our true reflection and acknowledge ourselves as being divine.

RITUAL

Here is a simple ritual for contemplation, an essential requirement for evolution and ascension and something which all seekers on a spiritual path should enter into at least 2 or 3 times out of every month if not once a week. It is a simple practice but it is powerful and potentially disruptive in regards to that sediment that we can drag to the surface, that we may not even know exists. Therefore it is essential in regards to any form of self enquiry or contemplation that you make sure that there is space in your life in order to process any negativity that may emerge as a result of this exercise. When we contemplate we stimulate a particular section of the brain known as "the Cave of Brahma". It is a central part of the cortex of the brain and in the meditation, in the ritual that will be given, this particular section of the brain will be stimulated. For some, as a result of this, there will be an odd sensation of vibration or even warmth within the head. This is quite natural and nothing to be concerned about but rather a good sign that you are entering into the right areas of brain rhythm and energy.

Make sure that you will not be disturbed, take the 'phone off the hook, close all the doors, turn off all interrupting sounds; radios, televisions, make sure that the space in which you are going to contemplate is as silent as possible. Light some incense if you would like and a candle of silver or white. Sit before the candle and take a few moments to centre and ground yourself. Breathe smoothly and evenly and bring yourself into the present moment. Allow any distracting thoughts to float freely through your head, acknowledging them but paying them no great mind or attention. Then in front of the candle trace the two interlocking triangles that form the hexagram or six-pointed star representing the co-joining of the lower and higher self and speak this invocation:

"Cassiel of the Seventh Star, I call your name and presence into this space, into my mind and heart. Great revealer of truth, Angel of contemplation and self enquiry, still the ripples of my mind, smooth the contours of my heart. Make this space a reflective mirror in which I might truly see myself at last. I ask these things of you in perfect love and perfect trust. So mote it be. Amen."

Now close your eyes and with your eyes closed, for a brief moment roll them upwards and inwards as if you were trying to look at your brow centre, and then relax the eyes. This simple physical gesture enables the brow centre to open slightly. The brow centre, the centre of perception, is used in self enquiry and contemplation. Now imagine, superimposed over the head, two triangles forming, one pointing up, one pointing down, overlapping on top of each other to form the hexagram. Don't concern yourself with their particular placement within the head. They are symbolic of energetic lines of connection that are being made within the brain between the pineal, pituitary and hypothalamus glands and the inversion of these lines of energy which will be instantly created in reflection. The symbol is enough to activate these lines of connection.

Once you have visualised this symbol now begin to imagine that your consciousness is reaching higher and higher above your head. It is rising like a rocket, like a shooting star, towards an enormous white sun. The white sun is your soul, your higher self. Once your consciousness has reached it the sun will begin to send down towards your body a powerful stream of white light. It flows in rippling rays of incredible brightness. It descends through your head and into your heart centre, opening the heart centre and allowing it to be flooded with light. At the same time the brow centre opens wider too and light emerges from this point also. You are enswathed with brilliant white light and with violet light from the brow centre and green light from the heart centre. At this point you may feel some sensation within your brain as the hexagramic connection is activated more powerfully.

Now in this state of alignment open your mind to contemplation. If you need to be prompted, if there are no issues that you particularly feel you want to contemplate at this moment in time, then use some of the simple statements of self enquiry: Who am I? Why am I here? What can I do to become enlightened? How can I better express my purpose for being? Mull these thoughts over in your mind. You are not seeking conclusion but rather contemplating these questions and it must be done in a focused and yet passive way, like a daydream, as if you were musing upon these questions.

Remember you are not seeking conclusions or answers. If they come all well and good but it is the act of contemplation that draws you closer to the truth and the truth always comes *to* you and is not created *by* you. Sit in this state for as long as you so choose to. Allow your contemplation to take you into a number of different places. Do not specifically hold it fast to one topic but let your initial investigation lead you into many different routes of contemplation and areas of self enquiry.

When your time draws to a close bring your awareness back to the heart and the brow, open wide with light streaming from them. Use your intention to conclude now, to disengage from the higher self, the soul, and allow the final remnants of light that it pours down through you to pass through you into your energy field. Feel your consciousness descending from your soul connection and simultaneously see and feel the brow and the heart chakra beginning to reset themselves. The hexagramic symbol in your head begins to fade and the vibration in your brain decreases. Take a few deep breaths and ground and centre yourself in the usual way, calling upon, finally, protection to surround you. Snuff out the candle and keep it somewhere safe so that you may always use only this candle for this exercise.

Make sure you are fully grounded before you enter back into your day by writing down some of the more interesting contemplations that you have had or drinking a cup of coffee or tea or glass of water or walking briefly out into the garden, into the air and grounding yourself fully into Mother Earth.

END OF RITUAL

This exercise will become very easy to master in time and its power should not be underestimated. Silence is a big part of the key to its success and any opportunity to enter into silence for lengthier periods of time will help you move automatically back into this space of contemplation.

It is only through self enquiry and contemplation that we can set ourselves free, free of the illusions of our life and free of the illusions of our world. It is only through silence and contemplation that we can contact the Divine, though there are many different ways of entering into this state and many different words for it. Prayer, meditation, using breath, the recitation of mantra, even using certain postures can trigger moments of contemplation and self enquiry. But do be aware that many of the things that can initially rise to the surface can be of a negative nature and therefore it may be beneficial to have someone to talk to about those things that have arisen that you may find initially difficult to come face to face with.

As the Angel who represents these great and mysterious powers, I am an Angel who is the fundamental presence for all those who seek to become enlightened and to ascend. Be then aware of who and what I am and call upon my presence and my power well. For the time being I leave you with my love and light, my truth and trust and peace.

ARCHANGEL LASSIEL

The Angel of Consecration

I am Lassiel, Angel of Consecration. The Angel of light who is the bridge of fire that enables the power of the Divine to enter into your world and make those things mundane divine in the Source's name. Consecration is a process which has up until recently been considered to be a power only held by the priests of your religious sects. The consecrations that they perform upon homes and sites, upon children and objects, an action that brings about the deification of a thing was considered to be a power that only the most holy could hold, only those who had been themselves consecrated by the Divine, ordained as priests of the Divine's law, light and truth. The truth of the matter is that this is not so. Consecration is a divine right and power which all hold and it can serve a very powerful and very valid function not only in the unfolding of the Divine Plan but also in regards to the safeguarding of people and places from the darker forces that exist within your sphere.

Let me then begin by explaining exactly what consecration is and how it works. Everything that is or was organic in nature, a tree, a flower, honey, water, even air, contains within it the Divine Presence. The Divine Presence expands and exists in all forms of reality, the seen and the unseen, the material and the non-material, right down to the deepest, darkest levels of your sphere. The Divine Presence in some things is more submerged and buried but can be invoked and awakened and consecration is one of the processes whereby this little miracle can occur. Now it is important at this early juncture to state that although inorganic materials, plastics and synthetics, do not contain naturally the presence of the Divine within them because they themselves were not created by the Divine, they do contain a small percentage of divine energy and presence because they were created by the creation of the Divine itself, by man and womankind. However, it is more difficult to consecrate inorganic materials and the quotient of divine realisation that can be brought about within said object is always less than that which can be liberated from within an organic structure.

The liberation then of the Divine within organic structures, whether they are living or dead, is done through the act of consecration, an act whereby this indwelling divine spark is accentuated and magnified, transforming the object energetically but also on a subatomic molecular level. The realms of the subatomic are only just being explored and understood by your scientists. There are many realms which their vision has not yet penetrated and there is much understanding which is still, at this moment in time, beyond them but they do comprehend that it exists and that in certain ways and at certain levels it defies the law of physics, that it is a realm unto itself with unlimited and infinite potentials and possibilities. It is here on this level that the Divine Presence resides, on the most subtle and the most simple. And it is this level which is instantly changed when this energy is liberated, when it is exploded like a nuclear force, transforming its own minute, internal universe into one more Divine realised, more active, more energised with the presence of the Source itself.

This affects the gross and molecular structure of the object it is true but in a way which, at this moment in time, cannot be measured by science but a way which *can* be felt by those sensitive amongst you. The act of consecration then makes something more divine. It liberates its internal divinity and makes it holy. This means that this object becomes aligned more greatly to the presence and the power of the Divine Source, becomes a conduit that holds divine resonance and that can be filled with divine power, holding more and more force inside it, becoming more and more aligned and connected to the true original source of divinity. The object itself in time then will take on certain divine powers; the powers to heal or inspire, the powers to align an individual who uses it to the holy presence of the Source or one of its many expressions and archetypes. It will magnify the intent of those who place their prayers upon it. It will become a focal point, a receptacle and a magnifier of all true intent, love, peace and desire.

In truth it matters not what the object is, whether it is chair or table or window ledge or whether it is a statue representing the Mother Mary. Though, of course, certain objects through their association and therefore their psychological link to the consciousness of mankind can more easily be recognised as divine. The consciousness and perception of mankind has a dramatic and powerful effect upon their surroundings and if they acknowledge the shape of something to be representative of the Divine in some form or another then they will enable that object to become more divine through their recognition and perception, they will anchor the divine energy, pull through the object more of the Divine's power and presence. Still, however, if an unfamiliar object is consecrated, sensitives will be able to recognise it and if it were adored and worshipped in the same way as a holy statute might be, it would in time take on the same attributes and powers.

Various religions would have mankind believe that only certain objects can be utilised in this capacity, certain symbols, forms, certain shapes and statues, certain images, but this is not so. As the Divine is in all things the Divine can be accentuated, consecrated, in all things also; in a tree living or dead, in a table or a chair, in a flower or a blade of grass, in those things natural and unnatural to man. The act of consecration then enables an object to become aligned and attuned to the Divine Source whereby it can become a conduit for this power and exhibit certain holy properties and abilities. Of course it is not only objects that are consecrated but indeed people are too when they are initiated or christened. This consecration holds a particular intent to purify and align the body, the mind, the heart, the soul, to the Divine so that they can be more connected, protected, guided and inspired by this presence and indeed, if the consecration or christening is done correctly it will have the desired effect. Whether or not the child, man or woman will choose to embrace the Divine Presence that they have been consecrated to is up to them. If they do, their consecration will become more active and empowered through their own act of self-perception and their own act of worship in this way. If they do not, then the consecration will remain but become disempowered in a sense. Of course too spaces can be consecrated, consecrated to the Divine, to the light, for a specific function; the worshipping of the Divine for healing purposes and so on. And when consecrated, that space if worked in will gather and build to it a positive and powerful energy which can be used for those purposes, magnifying and strengthening all that takes place within them and protecting the individuals inside from the darker forces that might seek to interfere with their good intentions.

Consecration then is an act of transformation. It is an act of bringing heaven to Earth, of allowing more and more of the

Divine's light to shine through. You might think then why do we simply not consecrate everything we come into contact with if this is our intention, to bring the Divine Presence more strongly into our physical reality. And you would be right in thinking that this is a good idea. Those who are strong in the light, who walk the path of the enlightened, who seek truth and love and enlightenment do become living conduits for consecration and their footfall will bring the Divine to the place that they journey into. Anything and everything that they touch, that they do, that they say, that they are, will be consecrated with the living light of the Divine; the words that they speak, the air that they breathe, the bed that they rest upon, the food that they eat. In certain religions people are asked to remove their shoes before entering into a holy space. People have often believed that this was as a sign of respect so that we would not bring the material world into the divine space but enter into it in a more humble state of grace. This is not true. The reason why Moses was asked to remove his shoes before entering into the presence of the Divine was so that he could be used as a lightening rod of consecration in order to bring to that space the presence of the Divine that communicated to him. When we enter into a space removing our shoes we do so in order to consecrate it with our light, in order to add to that space the individual essence of our divinity and to amplify its radiance and majesty. Each and every one of us has the power to transform the world around us, if we so choose. Others, of course, prefer only to focus on transforming themselves.

The act of consecration then is powerful magick. It has the capacity to bring the Divine closer to us: into the space in which we work and live, into our own bodies, minds, hearts and souls and into those objects that we would choose to use or focus upon as a point of worship and devotion, these objects then themselves becoming holy and powerful relics that can be passed on to others to aid and assist them after we no longer have need of them or after we have passed into spirit ourselves. Of course, it would be ridiculous to consecrate ridiculous things. Who is going to benefit from a consecrated fridge other than the person who eats the food from within it and it is far more appropriate for them to consecrate the food itself before they eat it than the receptacle that might hold it. We must respect this holy process as being just that, a sacred one, and not become dizzy with the possibilities of consecrating every small and ridiculous thing within our home or life. But if we apply a little practicality it would be easy to consecrate the glass that holds the water that nurtures the thirst of the sick. It would be easy to consecrate the sheets in which lie the ill and ailing. It would be simple to consecrate the air that carried the vibration of the teacher's teaching so that it may more efficiently conduct the light of the divine truth into the ears of the students who hear it. It would be appropriate to consecrate the tools that we use in order to perform the spiritual work that we perform.

Here then is a simple ritual for consecration that you can use upon objects, people or places. Once an object, person or place is consecrated it is marked by my divine fire. The divine fire serves as a bridge that aligns the person, place or object to the Divine Presence and evokes from within them the divine light. This light once activated frightens away the darker forces and presences and beings of ill intent that might seek to claim that person, place or object for themselves. It marks a boundary over which darkness may not tread. Of course, there are times when powerful dark forces seek to oppose the light but if a person, place or object has been consecrated then it has secured the protection of the Divine and if a battle ensues it will be one in which you have powerful light on your side.

Consecrating those places that have been polluted by darkness, by anger, fear and war, by murder, hate, torture and pain, is also a very valid, holy act. Reclaiming these withered patches of darkness to the light so that the fabric of your reality may be healed and whole is a good and virtuous duty and one that should be encouraged more and more amongst man. Often it is easy to think only of the living who suffer when such acts of horror occur but the world is living and therefore also needs to be rescued from its trauma and its plight. Consecration is a healing that enables this to be done.

RITUAL

Gather then the person or object that you would consecrate or take yourself to the place that you would consecrate or simply have a picture of that place or that place's name before you. Make sure that you will not be disturbed. Play some music, light and gentle, if you so require, or sit in silence. Light some incense of a high vibrational nature, frankincense, myrrh, lavender, and light a single white candle, placed upon the table, altar, shelf or floor before you with those things that you would consecrate. Have a small dish of salt and a small dish of water. First of all place the first two fingers of your right hand into the salt and say:

"Creature of salt, creature of earth, be cleansed and cleared of all impurity in the Divine's name."

Imagine your crown centre opening and a beautiful plume of white fire descending into it, flowing down through your head and neck, across your right shoulder and arm and down through your fingers into the basin of salt until it is ablaze with this white, fiery light. Take a few grains of the salt and place them into the water. Place your hands into the water and say:

"Creature of water, be cleansed and cleared of all impurity and pollution."

Once again visualise the plume of white fire descending into the crown, down through the head and neck, along the shoulder and down the right arm into your fingers and into the water where it mixes with the cleansing energy of the salt, doubly cleansing and purifying the water. Now say:

"I consecrate this water in the Divine's name. I consecrate it to light and love and truth."

Trace over the surface of the water an equal-armed cross, encircled. Make sure that you make the sign of the cross as follows: from above to below, from the left to the right and draw the circle clockwise and three times round.

Now bring your attention to the object, person or place that you would sanctify, that you would purify, that you would consecrate. Make a statement similar to this to the Divine:

"Divine Source of all light and love, I ask your aid in the consecration of this [person, place or object]. I call upon the power and the presence of the Archangel Lassiel, the Angel of Consecration, to aid me in this rite and work, purify this [person, place or object], sanctify this [person, place or object], consecrate this [person, place or object] to the light, to the divine love and to truth. I ask this for the good of all and to harm none. Let it then be so."

Sprinkle a little of the water on the person, in the place or upon the object and then draw the equal-armed cross, as previously mentioned, over it. Hold your palm face down as if you were pressing it against the symbol that you had drawn in the air and make this statement:

"Through light and enlightenment, through love and wisdom, through truth and knowing, I consecrate this [person, place or object] to the Divine. I purify this [person, place or object] in the Divine Light. I align and connect and invoke the divinity that exists outside and within it so that it is now and forevermore holy and sacrosanct."

As you say these words imagine the equal-armed cross becoming brighter and brighter with a burning white light. More and more of the fire descends into your crown, flows down through you and into the object, place or person until they are ablaze with brilliance. Hold this space for a moment. You will feel my presence. It will stand behind you. My wings will be as white fire and the brilliance of consecration will descend through me and into you and into the person, place or object. After a while say these simple words to conclude the ritual:

"It is done, it is so. So mote it be; amen."

END OF RITUAL

The water and salt that you have consecrated you may keep and use again. You may use the water immediately, sprinkling it upon your garden or within the space that you have used or placing it in a small bottle and passing it on to a friend. You will, of course, each time you perform this ritual of consecration need to begin with fresh water and you will need to once again purify the salt in case it has picked up any impurities since you last used it but you may use the same physical salt.

This act of consecration is relatively simple but incredibly powerful. You are participating in an act of transubstantiation, spiritual change, alchemy, transformation and magick. You are altering the fabric of your reality and drawing it closer to the Divine's presence. This is a powerful tool and one which must be honoured and used wisely and well.

Take then this gift. Use it wisely and well and know that you are an extension of the Divine and as such contain within you all the power of the Source. In love, light and truth I leave you. Blessed be.

ARCHANGEL ✦ JOPHIEL ✦

The Angel of Creativity

I am the Archangel Jophiel*. I am the Angel of Creativity and play, the Angel of light and joy, the Angel of inspiration and invention. I am the angelic muse who has touched the minds and hearts of many in order to inspire them to efforts of greatness. Some might consider my presence unimportant, they might find it odd to believe the Divine in all its infinite wisdom would create an Angel whose task would be to inspire mankind with creative endeavours. Some might believe that creativity has no place in the evolution of mankind, is unimportant when held in comparison to politics or religion or philosophy or the healing arts. But the truth is that creativity is key to all these things and more. Mankind/womankind are microcosms of the macrocosm from whence they came. They are small reflections of the great Source that was their home. They are, after all, cells that have been detached from the body of the great Divine and given independent existence. They contain within their primal essence a reflective nature, the Divine in embryo, a holographic matrix which contains within it all the unrealised, infinite potential of the Divine Source itself. They are expressions and reflections of the Goddess and God.

The Divine Source in both its matriarchal and patriarchal

---

* Pronounced Yophiel

139

forms is creative. The Divine Mother infinitely so, for it is from her and through her that all matter was brought into being. The Divine Father is creative in a more literal, logical and linear sense. The Divine Father is the architect and the Divine Mother the substance from which all things have been formed and therefore both these faces of the Divine are fundamentally creative in nature. The nature of mankind then contains within it the same creative impulses and tendencies. Women are more tied to the Divine Feminine, to her primary creative energies, and their desire and need to create is more integral and important in regards to their wellbeing and grounded expression here on Earth. Men are more connected to the linear, literal, architectural, strategic nature of creation which is found within the Divine Father himself. Creation for men is not so imperative in regards to it being directly connected to their health but nevertheless it is a primary part of their energetic being and pattern and therefore very important. Creativity then is a fundamental part of your society. Mankind tends to perceive it as being only within the arts that they employ their creative spirits; to create paintings and sculpture, song and dance, the skills of performance, writing, poetry and so on. But the truth is that the creative spirit is present in all areas: in politics, in religion, in philosophy and in science and spirituality too, for all of these areas require creativity in order for these new thoughts and theories to be invented and brought into being. Even spiritual development and unfoldment requires creativity in order for the medium or healer to interpret the signal that they receive when they open themselves to spiritual communication or the energy that they transmit as a healer. The manner, the way in which the words are spoken, the healing is given, is dependent upon creative thought and feeling in order for it to find its multi-faceted manifestation throughout the spiritual world.

Creativity within politics is evident not only in the positive ways but sometimes also in the negative. Creativity is required to set up political structure, to create political reform, but also unfortunately to create the illusions that are all too often woven to shield certain political agendas and to create powerful political figures that inspire trust and following. In philosophy creativity is obviously abundant in the way in which mankind has applied their thoughts to create a philosophical world of possibilities that enable mankind to draw closer to the true concepts of divine existence and to see the way in which the soul expresses itself through the spirit within the consciousness, unconsciousness and super-consciousness of mankind. Within science creativity has long been recognised as being the modus operandi of many great scientific minds. Einstein, Newton, the great scientists who have forged the basis for physical and chemical understandings, have brought forward their theories often through daydreaming, creative endeavours, rather than through mathematical and logical scientific calculation. It is usually the creative aspects of the brain that enable scientists to dare to imagine and begin to conceive the true nature of the structure and design of your universe rather than the more literal and linear calculations that provide the evidence for the wild fantasies that scientists dream into being.

Creativity then is an essential for mankind's health and for the creation of their world, for the structure of their civilisations and societies and the comprehension of the physical matter of the Earth plane. But there is much more to it than this. Mankind is endeavouring to emulate their creative source, to embody and example more of their true divine potential and being, and in order for this to occur they must embrace their true creative fire and use it with passion, not only upon their world but also upon themselves. They must strive to recreate everything in the image of their divine perception in order to bring that that is into alignment with that that is meant to be. They must recognise that their creative potential is not limited purely to ideas or to the mouldings of the materials of their world but also exists on a potential of divine reconfiguration whereby the creative powers can be employed to restructure matter in accordance with their own diverse desires. In the beginning in the ancient lands of Lemuria and Atlantis the Lemurians and latterly the Atlanteans initially had the power to reconstruct their reality through the power of their will alone. Granted the Atlanteans had a little help from the crystal skull collective, the Conclave, and the Lemurians benefited from the liberated Shekinah particles, the energy of creation that was so vibrant and free within matter at that time, but nevertheless it was their creative designs, their will, their energy to create that enabled them to reshape and reform the world around them in accordance with their needs and desires. The Lemurians did not build their towns and cities, they manifested them in much the same way that the Atlanteans drew crystals from the earth and raised and shaped them into their towers and spires.

Mankind possesses these potential powers but at this moment in time the vibration that exists within this world is far too harsh and heavy for it to be reformed and changed. The Shekinah energy at this moment in time is still constricted, though work is being done every day to release it from its confines so that matter may be re-informed by it to be more compliant. What mankind needs to do in order to prepare themselves for the time that will come when matter will more conscientiously obey their commands is work upon the liberation of their own co-creative powers. They need to recognise the potential that they carry inside themselves and to set it free. Do not mistake what I say here. Every man and woman who exists upon the Earth does not have to be a great artist or a great designer. Creative energies are not about artistic temperaments or capabilities, they are about imagination. Imagination is the capacity to conceive something which does not already exist, to conceive a solution to a problem. Each and every person has a practical, imaginative capability that they can draw upon in order to think themselves out of a difficult situation. Such power, if encouraged, can be used to recreate their society, to recreate their world into a new image, into a new form, and to recreate themselves also into a more enlightened and evolved body and nature.

The liberation of this creative potential is part of spiritual evolution and unfoldment, for it is a greater recognition and honouring and owning of the divine potential that exists within. And so the little ritual that I outline now is for people to use in order to liberate their creative potential. It is something that anyone can perform, whether they be artist or not, in order to aid in their personal evolution and transformation in order to draw them closer to their divine potential so that they can begin to employ their creative abilities in bringing about the manifestation of their own desires of the world around them in accordance with the Divine Plan, their life and themselves. But it is also a ritual that can be particularly used by artisans who are finding it difficult to overcome blockages or obstructions that they encounter along their creative path. It is a ritual that can be used to disrupt and disturb the creative blocks of the psyche and liberate inspiration from on high.

RITUAL

In the morning, before 12 noon, an altar is to be created, an altar dedicated to myself and the Angels of Creation. The altar itself should be creative, bearing colours that are light and optimistic, airy, positive and dynamic; blues, golds, yellows, violets, oranges; strong, bright, open colours. Upon the altar objects that represent creativity are to be placed; postcards of paintings, small sculptures, work that has been created by the individual, whether it is knitwear or patchwork quilts, whether it is a picture that was pieced together years ago with felt and buttons, something that represents the creative energy of the individual that they have liberated in the past. The altar must also carry a candle or two of colours that are connected to my energy; yellow, pale blue, emerald green and also some crystals that are connected to creativity such as rutilated quartz, smoky quartz and citrine.

The individual sits before the altar and centres themselves, they light the candle and any incense that they would like, an incense that is evocative of optimism and dynamic energy such as frankincense, ylang-ylang or patchouli and they invoke my presence and the presence of the creative Angels using these words:

"I call upon the presence and the power of the Archangel Jophiel, I call upon the presence and the power of the Angels of Creation. Hear my prayer, hear my invocation and enter into this space. Bless me with your presence. Bless my home, this sacred space, this sanctuary, with your light. In love I ask these things. Come forward then in peace and truth and trust. Angels of Creation, fill me with your light and joy. Cleanse and clear me of all obstacles and barriers that prevent me from accessing the well of my own creative spirit, my own inner potential to create in accordance with my divine inheritance. Angels of Creation, liberate and set the creative fire and spirit within me free. Align me to my source and let me be the bearer of my inheritance so that the creative fires may flow through and from me and enable me to hold this power, to set it free, to express it, into my world and into my life."

Visualise from on high the descent of a brilliant, golden-yellow flame. The flame descends into the crown and moves from this point into the body, through all of the chakras of the body, through the meridians and out into the subtle bodies and the auric field until the individual is ablaze with flickering, flaming, golden liquid light. The fire of creation burns away the blockages that prevent the person from being open to creation and inspiration. It moves through mind and heart, through body and spirit, enabling the person to connect with the creative potentials and essences of their soul. It also carries within it my breath, the breath of inspiration, that enters and burns into the centre of the mind and the heart, opening up the passageways to inspiration and the powers of the muse.

The individual sits within the light and fire of creation for a little while and then visualises it moving deeper inside them to their core, out of the range of their perception. This is the time for the individual to lightly and gently focus their awareness upon that situation that they are seeking to be creative in: a project, an endeavour, some area of their life, holding themselves open to the inspiration that comes from the Angels, from me and from the Divine Source, from their soul. They wait in gentle pause and then after a little while snuff out the candles and give thanks to the presence and the gift of the creative fire that has been given in a very gentle and general way.

END OF RITUAL

It is important for the individual to remain open to any

form of inspiration that may come to them within the next few days. It is important for them to give themselves opportunities to enter into creative repose. Creative repose is a state of gentle daydreaming where the mind is allowed to wander free into creative spaces. Sitting in one's garden, listening to music playing, walking in nature and allowing the mind to wander, allowing it to centre and settle itself upon the creative splendour of the world around us, entering into states of creative play.

Creativity is often best brought about when we break the rigidity of our structure, for it is not a linear attribute, creativity, but more lateral and therefore if we are going to bring something into manifestation we must not be too strict about it. We must not give ourselves strong boundaries and we must not place on to ourselves pressures that make it difficult for us to open up to the creative inspirations of the universe. Playing with colour and shape and form, with ideas on paper in a communicative way with someone whom we might bounce ideas off is the perfect way to allow creativity to flow freely and emerge. Play is essential in order to birth creative power and therefore opportunities for creative play must be given within the days following the small and gentle ritual that has been done.

The ritual is very simple. No more than the focused creation of an altar and an invocation and a little applied visualisation, a prayer, and yet it is very powerful. Creative potential lies within every cell of the body and within every particle of a person's energetic form. To liberate this by calling upon the creative fires of my realm can be fundamentally transformative. It can liberate a person to see their world in a completely different light, to reconfigure their life. It can open within them the portal that will allow them to bring about monumental manifestations within their reality. The creative fires of my realm are not to be misunderstood or looked upon as minor, for they are great and potentially world transforming.

It has often been my duty to appear in the minds and hearts and dreams of those who have been predestined to bring about powerful creative changes to your world. I am the muse Angel, I am inspiration, I am the ideas that descend upon the artist, I am the ray of sunshine that illuminates something that inspires a person to create. I am the synchronicity that enables a person to snatch music from the air or to come up with the political reform that will liberate a country. I am that moment of revelation, of realisation, when the light bulb comes on in the darkened mind and allows it finally to see. This is my presence and my power and it is has been more responsible for the reformation and changing of your world than you could ever imagine.

Creativity is a simple thing. It is something that we are taught to do from a very young age and yet as we grow it is often a power that we leave behind. We become pressured into creating things of beauty that aspire to the judgements of others rather than continuing to create out of pleasure and joy for ourselves and yet this is the essence, this is what we must strive to do. Embrace then your creativity, children of the Divine. Recognise that be you artisan or not, each and every one of you has the power to create. You are not seeking to create a "Mona Lisa" and or a "David", you are simply seeking in essence to recreate yourself in alignment with the image of your own true being. You are seeking to liberate your own creative tendencies and powers, which may not all be artistic in nature. You are seeking to open yourself to the inspiration of my presence and my power and by doing so to recognise your own divinity and god-like grace.

Go forwards then; create, play. Open yourself to the inspirations of your world. Dare to dream and believe that you can reshape and reform your life and the world around you in accordance with your vision. Know that in order for something to occur, first and foremost the inspiration for the idea of how to change it must be present. I am that inspiration and you are the individual who can receive it and make it real. In love and light then I leave you with my love, I surround you with my blessing and send you on your way.

The Angel
✤ of Light ✤

I am the Angel of Light, the Angel of illumination, the Angel of truth. First-born above and beyond all to guard and protect the power of light, the existence of light within this universe, within your world. The principles of light are clear and evident. They are about illumination, clarity and truth. Light enables us to see, to distinguish one thing from the other, to have knowledge of something's true form and shape, to navigate and steer. In the spiritual world, those seekers on the path often try to determine mystical and occult symbols in a very cryptic and complicated way where in truth the spiritual attributes and essences which are conveyed by phrases or images are evident and straightforward with regard to the image or word that is used to describe the nature of the energy itself. For centuries, for thousands of years, mankind has contemplated, has cogitated on the meaning of light and yet the symbolic interpretation is open and clear. It requires no complex understanding of metaphysical truth but a simple, innocent, wide-eyed comprehension of what the phrase truly means.

As the Angel of Light it was given to me to protect all those who work to bring the light of the Divine to Earth, to guide them and aid them by attuning them to the power and presence of the Divine Light itself, by monitoring over their attempts to commune with this force and by facilitating the procedures through which they might be used as conduits and vessels through which this radiance might pass.

It also falls to me to monitor the balance of light energy in the universe, to ensure that it does not become imbalanced in any way but remains in harmony with its counterpart, the presence of shadow, of darkness, that is required at this moment in time in order to sustain duality and polarity within your universe. The law of polarity exists here and must be obeyed until such a time as the consciousness of man is expanded sufficiently to be able to remove themselves from the lower limitations of universal law when the consciousness of man and the universe itself will be lifted into higher states of vibrational truth that will enable it to transcend the lower limitations of the laws of the universe that resonate in the lower frequencies of reality. Until such a time the balance must remain. And yet of course it is in the very nature of light and darkness to seek to consume one another and remain supreme and so although it is that the balance must remain, the light and darkness are continually and eternally at war with each other, seeking opportunities to grow, opportunities to consume, opportunities to triumph, opportunities to be the greater part of the balance.

There are also forces that exist, intelligences, that govern over the darkness, that have the same function that I play within your universe, to ensure that the darkness, that the shadow, does not become imbalanced in any way. My intelligence and the intelligence of my counterpart oversee these forces but are not part of them. It is our duty only to sustain harmony and to try to rein in the forces to which we are bound and prevent them from consuming each other in a disharmonious fashion. Everything that occurs in the macrocosm occurs within the microcosm too. Our existence is paralleled by the existence of governing psychological aspects of your own consciousness which seek to maintain a balance within your own being of the light and dark factions of your own mind.

Mankind has a natural predisposition towards goodness and positivity but there is also an element that exists within man that is dark and scurrilous also. This force, known as "the shadow self", known as "the id", contains within it all that mankind has been led to believe and see to be unscrupulous, dark and shameful within the personality and character of man; anger, rage, jealousy, fear, envy, vengeance, darkness, hate. Forces which have at times risen up in man and consumed him through war, through acts of bullying and belligerence, through dark times of control and despotism. However, this presence serves a function, as the darkness, as the shadow within your universe does also. It motivates and strengthens, it steers and guides in a negative way. It enables us to see more clearly the definition of light within our existence and helps us to transcend that that we know we must not become.

One of the first stages of personal development, of conscious expression of the spiritual mind, is a realisation of the existence of light and darkness within the self and within the world. Not the simple comprehension of preconditioning regarding what is considered socially to be acceptable or not but rather a deeper, inner, spiritual awareness of light and dark. An awareness of that that expands and reveals and exposes and that that consumes and clouds and veils. How hate and fear, how anger and suppression, how bullying and greed veil the truth, hide the light, consume the positivity, diminish the Divine and how light and education, how healing and love, how joy and optimism expand and open the possibilities, the probabilities, the potentials of existence and enable the Divine to be more known and seen.

Light is illumination, an unfoldment, an exposing of truth. In the New Age community, in the spiritual world, much is spoken of it and the term "love and light" used in order to express New Age greetings, positive energy and good thoughts. "Love and light" or "white light" is an energy which encourages unfoldment, encourages exposure, encourages growth and the unfurling of inner divinity. It is enlightenment; it is realisation and when sent with good intent can enable those who languish in illness or pain, in confusion or despair to see the true course that will steer them free from the situation in which they find themselves and enable them to find the courage, the connection to the Divine that they need in order to prevail. It is an energy which heals through education, which liberates through revelation and clarity. It is an energy that can transform all and any dark situation through knowledge and truth.

The truth that comes from light is not always of an external nature. Your reality is created by you yourselves and determined by your perception of yourself and the way in which you then enforce your reality to interface with your assumptions regarding your own nature and being. If you have accepted projections that have been placed upon you in your youth that you are unfortunate, foolish and unworthy then you will create for yourself a reality in which these things are reinforced and made manifest around you. If you are encouraged to believe yourself as being strong, wise, intelligent, worthy and good, then you will create for yourself an environment which will support and encourage you to continue to believe these things. Light sent works upon the individual, illuminates truth concerning themselves; enables them to see the true nature of their essence, to cast off the illusions of such conditioning projections, whether they come from parents or peers, teachers or friends, society, religion or politics. Light illuminates, through the individual, the world around the individual so that it can be seen for what it truly is and transformed through this seeing into something more appropriate and better. The love that accompanies light is the love of the Divine that provides the individual with the courage to see the truth about themselves and know that they can draw upon the loving essence of the Divine to find the power to change themselves and the world around them. The love that comes with light enables man to know that they are loved by God and as such not alone but always accompanied and held with their parents' care.

RITUAL

The following then is a ritual of love and light that can be sent to people, places or situations to aid them when we are unsure of what we should or can do, when healing is not enough, when the problem is so complicated that we do not know where to direct our energies, when the situation seems hopeless, when the individual in question needs a miracle in order to recognise the error of their ways or to be awoken to the beauty within their own soul. Try to obtain a picture of the person or some form of image that represents the place or situation that you would send the love and light to. A clipping from a newspaper, a photograph from a magazine or simply even the name of the person, place or situation written on a piece of paper. Have a candle, white, set in a holder and make sure that you have space and time to complete this ritual without being disturbed. Settle your environment, light some incense, play some music. Make sure that the fragrance is light; a high vibrational incense like frankincense or lavender or pine, like sandalwood or jasmine and ensure that the music is light too in volume and in its nature.

Focus your attention upon the photograph or piece of paper to which you would direct the light and love that you would invoke and muster. Light the candle and gaze a little while upon the light of its flame then speak these words:

> "I am the flame of the Divine; I am the flame of the Goddess and the God; I am their light on Earth, it shines through me. Light to illuminate, light to make things seen and known. Light to guide the way and reveal the truth."

Repeat this invocation two more times and then envision that within the centre of your heart a flame, not dissimilar to the candle flame, burns brightly there. Fold your hands in the traditional prayer position in front of the heart and as you focus more and more upon this flame let it grow within you. Let it expand. Let it become a column of fire that burns brightly through your being and shines brightly around your form, its aura and illumination burning and beaming outwards through and into your aura and into the space around you. Now speak this invocation:

> "I am the love of God; I am the love of the Goddess; their love made manifest through me, love to heal, love to reassure, love to realign, love to protect and guide. I am the love of the Divine."

As you speak these words, three times round in total, the light that shines from the centre of your heart becomes imbued with the softest of pale pink glows until you are a living flame of pale pink light. Now direct your thoughts to the person, place or situation that you would beam this love and light to. See that as your thoughts, your attention is directed to this place, person or situation the love and light streams from you towards them. This love and light comes from the Divine, expressed through you as the lens through which the energy is focused via your intent and will. It is limitless and infinite. It saturates the person and the situation. It saturates the place with its energy; illuminating, lifting, loving, caring, guiding and protecting, penetrating deep into the hearts, minds and spirits of those within your focus. Let yourself for a little while be lost in this intention, in this visualisation and finally, when the visualisation is complete, bring yourself back into your body, into your being, into your normal state of consciousness, allowing the light to return to the flickering candle flame within your heart and say these words of thanks and prayer:

"Great and powerful Divinity, I thank you for this opportunity to be used in service by the Light Divine to illuminate my world with love. All praise and blessing be to the Divine that is you and that burns in me."

With this, pinch or snuff out the candle, put it to one side and use it only for this purpose. Take some time to ground and centre yourself and go about your day.

END OF RITUAL

Your world is full of misconception and such misconception exists about me. I am Lucifer, the Angel of Light, the light-bearer, the Angel of great brightness, considered in Christian mythology to have been the Angel who started the war of Angels in heaven and was cast out by Michael into the dark pits of hell. In truth I was first-born of all and created from my light Melchizadek, who would create in turn Michael, the Angel of the Earthly Flame. Rather than being cast out from heaven for my rebellious nature I was, because of my love for light and for mankind, awarded the great responsibility and joy of monitoring over the light and dark within your dimension in order to ensure that there would always be illumination and hope. Mankind confuses truth, history distorts fact and those who are born in light sometimes are remembered in darkness. Mankind would do well to remember this, that history is not all that we would remember it as being and that we would do better to focus upon our present than upon a past which is uncertain and forgetful.

I am the Angel of Light and as such can be called upon to bring light into all situations. To your thoughts, to your feelings, to your work, to your world; to protect, to clarify, to illuminate and to reveal; this is the nature of my essence, this is the nature of my word. In love and truth I leave you then with this learning as I take my leave.

✦ THE ✦
CHERUBIM

The Angels of the Web of Love

We are the Cherubim, the Angels of Love, a collective born from the Divine to safeguard and represent the forces of love that exist in your universe. We have come to speak of love, to explain its true nature and course, to identify some of its mysteries and powers and to awaken your awareness of its presence in your being and in the world around you. Many people believe, falsely, that love is the ultimate power. It is not. It is second to the ultimate power but it is not the ultimate power in itself. Change is the greatest force that exists, evolution, a current that underpins all of existence and non-existence, which urges and steers everything to evolve and progress, to change and transform, to become more than that which it is. Love is subject to this power. It is encouraged and steered to change, to transform from its original state into a higher state of being, to become something beyond its original existence. Love you see is an energy, a force, and it has a consciousness of a kind, an intelligence. It is a field of conscious power that exists everywhere, in every time, in every space and like all other forms of energy it has degrees of frequency and vibration, forms of love which can be categorised and experienced. Many people believe that love is a single, solid experience, a single solid entity, but this is not so. Love exists in many forms, in many places, in many ways.

In the past, mankind has tried to understand the nature of

love and they have concluded that like is not love, that desire is not love, that lust is not love, that envy is not love. But these statements are not true. These emotions, these expressions *are* love; love in a lower form, love in a denser vibration but nevertheless they are love. In its highest expressions love is charity, mercy, compassion, love is unconditional and without limit. These are the higher octaves of the lower expressions of the energy of love. They are the evolutionary pinnacles of what envy, lust, desire and like can become. When humans encounter someone whom they begin to love, the experience of loving that individual is very different to the experience that they will have of loving that same individual after a certain passage of time. Some would say that the initial crazy love that emerges when two individuals meet each other is bound to fade and that what exists after it is real love. Some more cynical would say that love atrophies and dies as nature does and cannot exist in a prolonged relationship but simply becomes tolerance or like or comfort or security but that the love that is experienced at the initial onset of a relationship has died and faded away. It is true that love can die. It is true that some love is not meant to last, not only forever but for short periods of time. Much can be learnt from a short, powerful explosion of concentrated love which lasts no longer than a couple of days but it is wrong to say that the first blooms of love are not real, for they are. They are the spark, the ignition of the energy of love and they are powerful, they are potent and evocative. But it would be wrong to say that the love that follows is true love. It is simply another form of love and it would be wrong to say too that all love atrophies and dies because that is not the case. Some love is eternal and infinite. Some love does last forever but all love changes and is transformed by the passage of time and the powers of change. Nothing remains the same and although in the later years of a relationship the love that exists may not be pas-

sionate and powerful but more secure and dependable, it is
no less love than the love that was experienced at the beginning of the relationship. It has simply matured, changed and
transformed into something less intense but nevertheless
sometimes equally powerful.

Mankind has ensnared themselves in an illusion which they
know and experience to be false. They believe that relationships are meant to last forever, that marriage is meant to
exist for at least one lifetime, that when people meet and fall
in love they are meant to stay with that person until they
die. This kind of continuance is unnatural. No one can pre-
dict the future. No one can know by the first experiences
of love that they will love that person forever. People
change. Circumstances alter. Love matures and sometimes
people are drawn together in relationships to experience the
intensity of their love for a very short period of time only,
and then they are meant to go their separate ways in order
to experience other loves with other people. Because
mankind has placed upon themselves the limitations of this
illusion of monogamy and of the institution of marriage,
they have imprisoned themselves inside something which,
in their heart of hearts, they know not to be true but which
nevertheless they use to create karma for themselves when
this marriage relationship does not continue. Some people
would say that the state of marriages today reflects the lack
of morals and virtues within mankind and also mankind's
inability to work at a situation which does not immediately present itself as being perfect. Others might suggest that
as the consciousness of mankind expands and grows, they
draw closer to truths which they cannot clearly express or
understand inside their minds but which dictate their
actions. They know that they are not meant to be together
forever with the individual who they meet and marry. They
know that when the time comes they must part company

and seek other relationships, even if this means the dismant-
ling of the family unit. Some would suggest that the state of
marriage and divorce at this moment in time is an indication of mankind's liberated consciousness from the illusions
of the institution of marriage, a false perception perpetrated
by religions which seek to control, and that now they are
following the rhythm of their own soul's drum and being
led to truer and more accurate states of being.

Love can be perceived as a web of energy, a net that is cast
throughout the entire universe. Those points where the lines
on the net, where the strands of the web criss-cross, represent people. People are nexus points for love, points of
meeting. They hold the strands of many people's love inside
their hearts. The love of their parents and their children and
their friends, the love of their pets and the love that they
have for nature, the love that they have for happiness and
joy, for sensation; the love that they have for living and
laughing and being. Love you see is not something which
only exists between people but can exist between people
and animals and people and nature and people and situations
and people and objects and people and times and people and
truths and people and very surreal and insubstantial things
indeed. Love is a force which is not conditional but which
exists in all ways and in all places. This web of love ensures
that mankind stays connected. It is part of a thread which is
known as "the thread of commonality", the thread of connection that binds all people together through the common
factor that they have all been born from the same original
source, the Divine. It was the Divine who wove the web of
love in the first place and placed mankind within it at these
points of intersection so that mankind would be part of the
web and would help sustain it through the loves that they
would create and experience, through the loves that they
would express. But sometimes the web can be damaged. It

can be broken by hate and suspicion, by fear and envy, by jealousy, by rage, by prejudice, by spite, by malignancy, by evil, by darkness. The web is very robust and it can repair itself but when we exercise our prejudice against another, when we are frightened of a certain creed or race, when we hate a certain individual or a certain people, when we recoil in horror for what one person has done or many people have done, we endanger the integrity of the web of love and we weaken the commonality that connects us together. We isolate ourselves from our fellow man and from God and we strengthen the illusion of separation that exists which tells us falsely that we are alone.

If we reach out into the web, if we sense along its lines and fibres, if we acknowledge and affirm that love exists within each and every thing that exists, within every conscious living life form and every unconscious living life form too, then we will help reweave the web around us. There is no man, no woman, no child who exists upon the Earth who has not known love, who has not been loved, who has not loved, who has not experienced in some shape or form love. Maybe not by a human being but by the Divine Source or for nature, for light or life, for joy or food or peace or security or comfort, by someone whom they have never known, by someone they have only ever seen in a fleeting glance. Each and every person, the darkest and the lightest soul, has known love and this connects and aligns us together, this holds us in a state of commonality and unity as one. This enables us to transcend and cross the barriers of prejudice and fear. This enables us to progress towards a point of unconditional love whereby we can love the light of the spirit and the soul that burns within the darkest human being by acknowledging that there is something that we share and that that is our source and that that is the presence of love within our being.

Mankind might not want to think that terrorists and rapists and murderers and paedophiles have love inside them, but they do. Likewise mankind might not want to think that these people are divine in essence, but they are. We must not judge the actions of an individual because we do not know what caused them to become the person who they have become. What we must strive to see is the light and love that burn inside them and to align with this to rebuild the bridges that have been broken out of loathing and fear so that we may all be one again. Here is a small ritual to aid in the reparation of the web of love, to be done whenever there are incidents of despair or horror that take place within the world that harm the web, a simple thing that you can do, and you can do alone, to aid in the distribution and repair of the existence of the power of love.

RITUAL

Begin by bringing your focus to your heart centre. Feel it in the centre of your being and imagine it as a spinning Catherine wheel of emerald green and pink light, like a flower opening or spinning, bright and shining and new. Now think of someone whom you love: a friend, a parent, a sibling, a dependant, a child, someone whom you love. A stream of light is illuminated; a thread that emerges from your heart and connects you to the heart of this one that you love. When you illuminate this thread by thinking thoughts of love in the direction of this individual, this individual consciously or unconsciously will feel this energy and they will send threads of love back to you too. This reinforcement of the love that you share for each other will illuminate other threads of love from your heart also and they will automatically be instigated. Light will begin to emerge as many threads from the heart outwards to all those people in your life whom you love, whether it be greatly or

whether it be only very small, and very soon you will see
that you are part of the web of love, a point on this web
with many lines emerging from the centre of your heart
outwards to your friend and to your other friends, to those
other people that you love, and that the same emerges from
your friend's heart too, that this simple, single act of thinking about someone whom you love has instigated the illuminating of the whole network of love that radiates outwards into the world, illuminating other hearts and activating their own loving energies also.

Now acknowledge, as you ponder this great inter-tangled
web of love and light, that some of these strands enter into
dark hearts. The hearts of those people who, through their
actions or through the way in which they are being judged
or seen by others, have become isolated from the web and
isolated from the Divine's love. The light that enters into
them now illuminates the darkness of their hearts also and
triggers threads shining brightly from their own beings out
into the world; maybe not as many as your own or your
friends' but nevertheless these threads illuminated in this
way help reweave and connect them to the web.

Now take your consciousness higher and be aware that at
the top of this web the strands of light all interweave and
plait together and join into one source, one raging point of
tremendous and infinite light which feeds all the threads
and all the points contained within it: the presence of the
Divine's love, which is infinite and eternal, which rains
down upon mankind and holds us all within its care. Now
let this impression go and breathe.

END OF RITUAL

This simple act of loving each other sets off then a chain

reaction, which spans the globe, which interacts with every other human heart and helps the world exist in love. What we do within our own world and for ourselves has macro-cosmic connotations. The chain reaction of loving another single soul radiates outwards into the planet and beyond and strengthens the web of love together. If then each day we could take time to think one loving thought, one single loving thought, we would reinforce and illuminate the web of love and help hold the world in love forever.

We are the Cherubim, the Angels of Love. Hear our words and ponder on our truth. In light and love we leave you in its care.

The
SERAPHIM

⟡ The Angels of the Weave ⟡

We are the Seraphim, many in one, a collective of Angels bound together as a community of consciousness. We are high amongst the most high, radiant beings beyond your imagination, sometimes envisioned as six-winged and six-armed weavers of the fabric of reality. We were created by the Divine Essence in order to aid in the manifestation of the realities, not only your physical world but also those other planes that exist above and below it. To aid in the creation of this space under the guidance of the Demiurge, the architects of existence, but also to maintain and repair the fabric of all that is. You, of course, are part of this fabric. You exist as part of this energy, part of the interplay of power that radiates outwards from all things. Part of the connection, part of the plan; part of the essence of your universe and your presence here, your existence is integral and required for everything to be.

Let us then explain that your universe is not exactly as you imagine it to be. Your perceptions are largely induced by suggestion and also your consciousness' capacity to interpret those things that are in truth beyond its own capacity. The consciousness forms images that are safe, enabling you to see the all contained within the one. But in time, as the consciousness expands, your vision changes too and you begin to see more freely the truer nature of the universe and acknowledge more clearly the interplay that exists between all those things that are held within it.

Imagine then that the Divine, the ultimate Divine, is a canvas upon which your reality is painted. A canvas is constructed from many tiny threads woven together to create a plateau upon which paint is placed in order to form a picture. The picture upon this canvas is your universe, your galaxy, your world and you. The canvas is the Divine Presence that permeates all things and the thread of the canvas is the universal weave, the web, the loom, the structure of existence that we are guardian and patron of. It is our duty then, our responsibility, to maintain a presence of awareness over this fabric and ensure that when it becomes damaged or torn or worn it is repaired. We have power over the physical universe, though sometimes use physical beings in order to affect this reparation when it is most economical to do so. Sometimes the fabric within your universe is damaged by natural things, emissions of energy and light which cause the fabric to rip and tear. A hole within the fabric of your universe becomes a portal, a "wormhole", that leads to other realities and can create dangers in a sense of things being drawn into them and drawn out of them that are not meant to journey away from your universe or into it from other universes that lie beyond.

There are other things too, unnatural in their design, that can cause holes to occur within the fabric of your space. Emissions of energy created by mankind that have worn away the robust nature of your existence; electromagnetism, certain sonic frequencies, x-rays and radiations but also anger, grief, war, greed and pain. These things, of course, are meant to exist, they are part of your experiential process that leads you eventually to a point of comprehension and evolution but when they occur in concentrated ways outside of the flow of the Divine Plan they can cause danger to the fabric of the web and create tears and holes within your universe. Particularly when these things occur not in accordance with integrity but outside of it can damage be done. Integrity is right action, not necessarily right action that occurs for the greater consciousness of man but right action which takes place in accordance with the consciousness of the individual. This right action does not cause damage or distress to the fabric of reality, which is dependent upon integrity in order to be maintained, but when an individual brings about an action not born from belief or truth but out of ego, greed or desire, when they proclaim that they do something in the name of the Divine but in truth are acting from their own egocentric point of will they cause a rent within the fabric of existence through this blasphemy, through the contrition that occurs from them saying one thing and yet meaning another. Truth is the foundation of all and when we operate outside of truth we damage not only ourselves but also the fabric of the world in which we live. endangering ultimately the universe itself. That is why honesty to the self and to others is so important, because of the damage that occurs in the universe and through the intricate, delicate filaments of light frequency that bind us all together as one.

The connection that exists between you is a connection that flows through the thread of reality. The threads bind together all things and all people, binding them as a whole, as a oneness. But the threads in particular bind individuals to those people, situations and places closest to them that are linked through commonality. This is the way in which the web expands from a single point. An individual is bound to people and places and situations around them that they have a likeness to and those people are bound to others who they have a likeness to also, creating from these single points of light a myriad of web-like patterns that radiate outwards to create the whole. It is this likeness, this commonality that connects us to everything, making us all part of the one great body of reality here. And this web, though particularly contained within limited space and time, extends into the higher realities of the seven spheres, connecting us to guiding presences, Guardian Angels, archangelic patrons, patron Masters and Cosmic Ascended Masters, God-forms and beyond. This web flies freely into the limitless spaces of existence, reaching ultimately and always back to the Divine Essence and Ultimate Source.

Mankind, awoken and spiritually aware, has always acknowledged the concept that they are one, psychologically acknowledging that the collective unconscious is an indication of this truth. They therefore have acknowledged and brought forward through their religious practices the true awareness that what we do to ourselves or another affects the whole and ourselves. That our anger focused towards those around us will ultimately affect us ourselves through reflection and that our anger focused towards ourselves will radiate outwards and affect the all. Holding this concept as a truth we must therefore contemplate that our own actions towards ourselves must enter into a state of balance if we are to live within a balanced society and world and that our actions towards others too must be kindly in order to promote kindness, tolerance, love and understanding. The macrocosm is a mirror of the microcosm. What we do within it is reflected inside us and what occurs inside us is reflected outside of us also. But also bearing in mind that our web starts from us and radiates out initially to those people who are connected to us through likeness we must acknowledge that our actions towards ourselves can affect those people who we hold dear and the community in which we live also. Therefore if you find it difficult to be kind towards yourself for your own sake, think how your actions towards yourself will affect those around you whom you love and bear in mind that the responsibility that you carry as an enlightened and awoken person is not only towards yourself but to all those others who you have connected and aligned yourself with.

Now, of course, this knowledge should not replace your consideration for yourself. Everything must begin with yourself but you can use this knowledge as motivation to try and correct the imbalances that exist within you, to inspire you to heal yourself and become whole. And it is to this effect that we would bring forward our ritual today to aid you in this endeavour. This ritual calls upon our power to align you to the higher templates that exist that may bring you greater harmony and balance by calling upon the energy of your perfect self, your higher self, your soul, to align the imbalanced and confused aspects of your personality and being, in order to bring you peace, harmony, clarity and truth. This ritual takes the form of a small meditation.

RITUAL

Take yourself then to a quiet place. Light incense and a candle and ensure that you will not be disturbed. Relax. Seat yourself comfortably, breathe deeply and relax. We will use simple visualisations, not actual representations of the truth but simple images in order to help you become better aligned. With your eyes closed envision before you, sitting in the same position in which you sit, a double of your being. The double, however, is more perfect than you. It is formed from light and shines with an iridescent star-like glow. There are no lines upon its face, there is only a gentle smile and a sign of great health, wellbeing, great harmony, great happiness and peace.

Open your mind's eye to this doppelganger. See them as they truly are. You may catch glimpses of them robed. You may find that their features blur and shift and that they show you other faces, the faces that you have worn in previous lives. You may find that they exhibit different qualities that you may not at first understand. Do not fight the impressions that you receive but simply see this representation of your soul, your higher self.

Now open your heart chakra and extend your palms so that they face towards the doppelganger before you. The doppelganger does the same and a tension builds in the air between the two of you. At this point our presence is invoked by simply intoning our name, "Seraphim". The energy of the Seraphim enters into the space, activating, aligning and enabling you to see the lines of connection that exist. A line of connection powerful and bright radiates from the centre of your heart to the centre of the heart of your soul. Other thinner, less illuminated lines radiate out from the centre point of your being into the world around you but it is this central line that you are focusing your attention upon. A transmission begins to occur, a flow of power. It moves slowly, like liquid molten light through your being, aligning heart and mind and body and soul, clarifying, strengthening, repairing, aligning; healing. It moves deeper and deeper into the essence and core of your being until you are illuminated from within; until you are aligned; until you are perfected; until you are cleared. Sit and allow this process to occur. In time you will notice that it has come to an end and that the doppelganger before you has disappeared. You have become aligned to your soul and the imbalances and kinks within the subtle bodies and states of consciousness of your being have been repaired, healed and corrected for the time being.

Now radiate this energy outwards into the greater world around you. See the bright light radiating through the intricate array, the intricate lines of power that connect you to the greater macrocosm. You are now taking the energy that has been given to you as a blessing from your soul into the greater community. You are allowing the peace and alignment that you have achieved to radiate outwards into the world, into the hearts and minds and souls of those who are close to you, linked through love. You are bringing about a healing to the community and world around you. Let this energy then flow and after some time bring your awareness back to the centre point of your being. Give thanks to the soul and to the Seraphim. Take a few moments to return yourself to normal consciousness. Open your eyes and return.

END OF RITUAL

This simple practice can be repeated as many times a week as you need to. It will enable you to enter into greater communion with your higher self, to gain greater stability and enlightenment regarding trying situations and difficulties, to receive healing and to in turn reflect that healing out into the world, into your community and society and towards those around you that you love. It is a powerful light and a powerful way of serving the greater good by serving the self.

The final thing then that we would say to you is this. As we have detailed, the fabric of your reality can be damaged by a number of things. These things at this moment in time cannot be fully eradicated but work can be done to strengthen and repair the fabric around these occurrences, whether they are wars or tragedies, whether they are electrical substations or places that are experimenting with energies that are potentially dangerous to the universe, whether they are medical treatments or people who have been treated in this way, there are ways in which you can help us to heal these places and these people from the potential damage that they have incurred.

This way is very simple, the Divine often favouring simplicity to bring about great miracle. Simply envision these places or take yourself to them physically and intone our name. Intone the name "Seraphim" at least three times, clear and bright and strong. You may intone the name more than three times or you may chant it as a mantra but whilst you do so you must surrender yourself to us to be used as a conduit through which we can pour the healing energies that are our power into the fabric of your world and repair that that has been damaged there. By intoning our name whilst holding on to another you will give us the opportunity to repair the fabric that constitutes that person's existence in this reality, if they have been subjected to electromagnetic or x-ray energy, and you will heal their connection to the universe around them. Concentrated exposure to negative energies of this nature can cause a deterioration in their connection to the universe, causing them to feel lost on their spiritual path, causing them to feel tired, hopeless, disconnected from God, the intonation of our name being able to repair these breakages and sustain them with new life and energy, taking away these symptoms and healing them once more.

Remember then our presence, our power and our importance. The connection that exists between you and the universe is responsible for aligning you to the guidance of your higher self, your guides and your patrons, to connecting you to your spiritual path and enabling synchronicity to flow into your life. If you experience a loss of any of these things then it may be that through some situation you have become disconnected from the filaments of light that join you to these forces. Remember then our name and our power to resurrect these connections and alignments.

We are the Seraphim, beloved light-bearers of the Divine, created to aid and sustain you and always here to lend our many hands to the greater cause. In light and love and truth we take our leave.

❖ THE ❖ ELOHIM

The Angels of the Web of Time

We are the mighty Elohim, the Angels of Time and No Time. We are the Angels of miracle and faith. We are the Angels clustered together like stars within the night sky, who have, since before the beginning of creation, been given the task and duty of monitoring over the energy of existence and occurrence which is known to man as "time" and the barriers and veils which separate the past from the present and the future. We form part of those angelic hierarchies created from the consciousness of the Divine before the manifestation of physical reality and limitation and therefore, unlike all those other Angels who exist within the continuum of Angels that reside within limited space and time, were not born from Melchizadek, the womb of the Divine Source, who is in himself a conduit and portal between the dimensions which we inhabit and the dimensions of reality that you have come to know as your own. There are others akin to us who exist within these higher spheres, collectives of Angels who have never known existence in the limited realms of being: the Thrones, the Principalities and Mentalities, the Divinities, Angels of great power and majesty whose duties and responsibilities far exceed the clear comprehension of mankind, that are infinite and surreal in nature. Our influence upon your dimension, upon your world, is such because of the way in which time so

174

defines the nature of your living and because our essence and our energy are required for all miracles to occur within your space, topics which we will discuss in a little while. First, however, it is more important for us to more clearly define the nature and role of our being, as can be best described to you, and also to provide you with some understanding as to the nature of time itself.

Time is an essence, an energy, a solution. Imagine a glass of water in which is placed a stone. The water is coloured by natural dye so that the stone cannot be easily seen. The water itself represents the energy of time. Time is a solution in which reality rests. The stone is matter, the physical dimension. It is completely surrounded and sometimes suspended within time's energy. Time permeates the stone, permeates matter and has an effect upon it although largely it is invisible and unseen. The colouration within the water is that part of time that influences matter in a more direct form. It is the piece of time in which matter rests which obscures it and holds it, which contains it. It is the present which rapidly becomes the past and which to pasts long gone is the future. The energy of time, which we are master and guardian of, is a force which is not completely understandable by man. Mankind, who lives within time, tends to perceive it as a straight line. They perceive history as having already occurred. They perceive the present as being an ever-elusive moment which passes as soon as it is entered into and they consider the future to be something which is yet to be written or created, an unseen landscape that lies ahead.

The truth of the matter is that time is concurrent, the past, the present and the future existing simultaneously as one. Time is not a straight line but rather a spiral or a coil, one circle or circuit of the coil being the past, the circuit or circle that lies beneath it the present, the circle or circuit that lies beneath that the future. Although the past, the present and the future are separated by space which we term as veils of energy, they are connected and concurrent. They take place simultaneously. Although an individual may journey through their own life stream and experience from the present moment their own past and their own future, that which they have journeyed through is not finished but continues to exist and that which lies before them is not waiting to be born but has been born, waiting for the individual to enter into. This perception of time makes time travel possible and an individual can easily slip from one ring of the spiral to another, moving from one parallel point to another parallel point and encountering a piece of an individual's past or a piece of an individual's future much more easily with this diagram than with the diagram of time being linear. Time being concurrent, being cyclic in this nature, becomes almost a diagram of parallel realities, which in essence it is more akin to.

It is our duty as Angels of time to monitor over the veils that exist between the past, the present and the future, to ensure that these concurrent loops do not merge or mingle or fall and collapse in together as one. The solution of time that we have spoken of is the veil itself, a woven fabric of energy that separates moments of temporal activity. The veil, the solution, the weave that separates these occurrences can become thin, the membrane punctured, and moments of the past, the present and the future bleed together into one current existent point. Although this happens rarely it has been known and still in certain places is experienced. Alerted to this aberration of nature it is our duty to repair it before it causes too much harm. But the structure of time becomes ever more dubious what with mankind's discovery of certain energies which impair the fabric of your temporal reality. Electromagnetic frequencies, harmonic energies, microwave radiations, nuclear forces, have all contributed to weakening the fabric of time in areas that have been bombarded with these powers. It becomes more difficult for the Elohim to fulfil their function, to perform their task and to repair the fabric when it becomes so increasingly endangered by mankind's persistent abuse of its existence. Of course, man might proclaim that as they do not know that such forces create such dangers, they cannot be held accountable and responsible for their actions. But the Divine cannot be accountable for that which mankind has forgotten or lost. These mysteries and truths were once taught to mankind and simply because mankind has chosen no longer to believe in them, to suppress or bury them, to squander this mystery and truth, does not mean the Divine is responsible for such ignorance, arrogance and presumptuousness. Mankind must now suffer the consequences of their meddlesome attempts at scientific discovery by coping with the possibility that in the future they may be confronted with temporal collapse in certain places.

Of course, whilst it is still possible, the Elohim will play their part in repairing the fabric of time and sometimes have called upon the assistance of mankind to do so too by utilising them as mediums and conduits through which the forces and spirits of time can act in order to repair the damage to fabric here on Earth. There are mantras, spells. There are intonements and dormant energy centres within the body of man which can be activated to do such things as the reparation of these veils but it is not these things that we have come to speak of now.

We have come to speak of another of our functions, as Angels of faith and miracle. Miracles are uncommon occurrences. They are situations whereby unpredictable and unlikely events occur as a direct result of a petition to divine forces for aid. Some people would claim that life itself is a miracle and there is some truth in this but this is an allegorical and poetic description and use of the word, the true use being more that which we have given, more that miracles are manifestations that occur directed by the Divine's will in accordance to prayers or requests made by mankind. Miracles occur outside of normal space and time. They do not flow in accordance with nature. We must not mistake a miracle for a working of magick. A working of magick utilises and incorporates natural forces to achieve its end. There is nothing natural about a miracle. It defies nature, occurs outside of time. Its manifestation does not necessarily always flow in accordance with what has been written but can sometimes be a spontaneous event which creates a rewriting of history, a rewriting of the past and the present.

Miracles require a number of ingredients in order to occur, the first of these being a request. A request for a miracle is often given through prayer, though sometimes can be delivered through simple concentrated intent. The miracle then is approved by the Divine Intelligence, the Supernal Light and is only granted if it flows in accordance and in sympathy with the Divine Plan and will not adversely affect another person's free will or life purpose. If it is then agreed that the requested miracle should take place, then powerful forces are brought into play in order to ensure that the miracle will be made manifest. One of the things that is required in order for a miracle to occur is faith. Faith is invisible and blind trust in the infinite and Divine Presence. Faith is not trust which has been achieved through the proof of existence of the Divine. This form of faith is different from the faith that is held by an individual who has had no concrete evidence of the Divine Presence itself. Faith in the invisible is born out of an inner knowing, an inner com-

prehension of that that has not yet been seen or confronted. Faith in the invisible, blind trust and knowing, creates a
portal within the petitioner of the miracle that allows the
miraculous to occur. The manifestation then of the miracle
requires petition and faith and thirdly, the presence of two
particular bodies of Angels who can enable the miracle to
manifest on Earth through the manipulation of certain
limited energies. One of these bodies of Angels is ourselves,
the Elohim. We are required to warp and alter the effect of
time upon the Earth to create a pocket of no time. No time
is a dimensional reality which exists beyond limited space
and time. Here anything and everything is possible because
this space is not subject to the forces of limitation within
manifest reality. The universal laws do not apply. Second, the
Malochim, the twins to the Elohim, who are the planning
Angels of the universe, who are the builders of your reality,
are required to reweave certain strands of energy in order to
make the miracle manifest. To suspend and alter certain
limiting universal laws; to rewrite the molecular structure of
physical matter; to replace and alter the encodements of natural energy which are in existence in order to ensure that
the miraculous happening can occur.

Of course, sometimes people say that miracles occur spon-
taneously and are not consciously requested through prayer
or intent. But this is not exactly so. Miracles are *always*
brought into manifestation through desire. The desire may
not be spoken. It may not be voiced. It may not even be particularly conscious but it is always the instigating force of
the miraculous occurrence. Many things that occur within
your reality are attributed to miracles when this is not so.
The seemingly miraculous properties and powers of icons
and figures which represent various divine beings are often
considered to be miraculous in nature. This is not the case.
Figures which are used as focuses for worship, icons which

are used as windows into the divine realms, are simply that; pockets that open up within reality in order to allow other-world realities and their energies to be made manifest on Earth, grounding-points for higher vibrational light and presence. The manifestation of the tears of the Virgin Mother, the manifestation of miraculous growth or movement of an icon is *not* a miracle in the sense of something occurring outside of time, something which requires the Malochim to reweave reality or the approval of the Divine Consciousness but rather simply a manifestation of energy pulled and anchored through a physical object. Miracles performed by *people* are sometimes not necessarily miraculous in nature: healings, prophesies, these things are all part of mankind's extended craft, their own co-creative divine power. Miracles such as the feeding of the 5,000 with loaves and fishes are indeed true. Such peculiar, unnatural occurrences which defy human law, which have no explanation, which are not connected to an iconic object or figure, which are not part of mankind's innate, co-creative, supernatural power, are most definitely miraculous.

Mankind then is the initial portal that allows the miracle to occur. Mankind's prayer, mankind's wish and desire and mankind's faith enable the manifestation of the miracle to happen. Often it is the case when an individual prays for a miracle and witnesses one that their faith alters because their belief is no longer built upon blind understanding of Divine Presence but rather because they have seen evidence of the Divine in action and therefore the individual after this point becomes incapable of being the portal through which a miracle can manifest. But some, however, irrespective of what they see, are untouched by this proof and concentrate only on this inner knowing of God's presence. This state is known as a "state of purity", a "state of true grace"; the concrete awareness of a Higher Intelligence which is not forged from proof of existence. Individuals who hold this awareness of the Divine are powerful and holy beings who enable a particular aspect of the Divine Presence to be made manifest and anchored here in reality.

You may wonder why we have come forward. You may wonder why we have felt there is need for you to understand the principles and mechanics behind miracles. Why it has been important to reveal the cyclic nature of time. We cannot provide you with rituals or systems for creating miracles. There is no guarantee behind them and we cannot provide you with information regarding how to manipulate time, for this knowledge is not meant for man yet. But what we can provide you with is this: the Divine is a presence which exists in the universe around you but also a presence which exists within your being. Each and every thing that exists was created through and from the Divine and as such is an expression of it and as such contains on an embryonic level, on a nucleus level, a part of the Divine Essence itself. As such it is possible to know the Divine without proof of its being by turning within and feeling within ourselves and knowing within matter the resonant existence and expression of Divine Light. This then is the ritual that we would give to you. This then is the conclusion that comes from everything that we have spoken of.

RITUAL

Take yourself to a place where you will not be disturbed. Give yourself some time within this space to perform this ritual at leisure. Ensure that there is nothing that you have to rush from the ritual to achieve, as during the ritual, time will be suspended and you may find that you journey out of the ritual having passed through a short space of time or a great deal of time. Light some incense, play some soft and gentle music, make yourself comfortable. Prepare for your-self a simple altar, a cloth of white or violet and a single white candle. Light the candle and pray using these words:

"This light is a mirror. It turns my gaze inwards; past the body, past the bone, past the blood, past the flesh, past the mind, past thoughts and worry, past the heart, past feelings of concern. Into the light, mirrored by the light, into the Divine carried within, this light is a mirror that allows me to journey into the heart of God."

Repeat this invocation twice more. Pronounce it slowly, methodically and in rhythm. Concentrate on the words and let it turn your mind inwards. As you journey into the cen-tre of your being, close your eyes and release all awareness of your form and your surroundings. Focus with your mind's eye upon a light at a distance and imagine yourself floating closer and closer to it, a discarnate presence being drawn to the light of the Divine Source within. As you approach the light, dissolve yourself into its consciousness. Rest within this blank whiteness and let the body and the voice of the Divine speak to you of its wisdom and its truth. Here aligned to the Divine, miracle *can* occur. Here aligned to the Divine, anything is possible. Here outside of time all and everything can be seen and known and the Malochim are at your disposal to reweave the nature of your life. Here aligned to the Divine the world and your existence lie before you like a map and the direction that you must take can be clearly seen.

After some time you will feel the pull of your body, the ache of your bones, the chill in the air, the sounds outside of the room and you will slowly disengage from the light and jour-ney backwards through the vast expanse of darkness, back into your form. Once you do, open your eyes and take care to ground and centre yourself appropriately before extinguishing the candle and concluding the ritual. You may find that little time has passed or that a great deal of time has drifted past you. You may find that the enlightenment that you have received will quickly fade from your consciousness and therefore it may be important to record it fast. Whatever may have occurred, this alignment to the Divine will alter and change you and you will from this point on become more attuned to the presence of the Divine within you and within your reality.

END OF RITUAL

We are the Elohim, the masters of time, Angels of faith and of miracle and belief. We are the unseen weavers of the web who spin the beginning thread of your lives, measure it as you grow and journey and break the thread only to reweave it again in the new lifetimes that you exist in. We are everywhere and everything, eternal and infinite, Angels of the Divine.

MOTHER MARY

✧ Divine Love ✧

I am Mary, Lady Ascended Master, bringer of peace and wisdom, Lady of Order and custodian of truth. I speak on those topics concerning the Divine Mother and the omnipresence of the Divine's love for all that exists within reality, within the material universe including, of course, this beloved planet and mankind. I speak here amongst this collection of wisdom brought forward by the angelic continuum because of my relationship to the angelic kind, because in the past I have been considered to be the Queen of Heaven by various religions and also considered to be archangelic in status in the higher spiritual realms. I have come in part to clarify this, to clarify my connection to the angelic continuum and to speak of Angels from the perspective of Master and to illuminate in regards to that truth which is a principle of the angelic ingredient, the power of God's love.

In truth I am not an angelic being. I have not been raised to this status. Such transformation is impossible. When one is created as a human soul one remains human and cannot be elevated to the status of an angelic being. To do so would mean that the soul would have to cross the streams of incarnation and existence, the streams of being, and not only is this practically impossible but it is also unnecessary and would carry no relevance or purpose. My connection to the angelic continuum is through my ancestry, is through the nature of my soul and the fact that it was created with contributions from certain angelic forces, making it in essence that that would be more accurately described as a Nephalim soul in nature. But this channelling is not one which has been brought forward in order to detail the complex consistency of my spiritual ancestry or origin but more to focus upon that issue that is primarily relevant to mankind at this moment in time, the presence and power of love upon the planet.

My connection to the angelic continuum transcends the nature of my soul's origin and is connected to the principle of love through the Divine Mother. The Divine Mother, the Universal Mother, the Goddess, is an expression of the Divine Source, a polarised expression that occurred when the Divine placed a part of itself into limited space and time at the beginning of all. That part that was placed into limited space and time became divided, subject to the laws of this material universe, became diluted and dissected, transposed into varying lower, denser expressions of its one true harmonious self, one of these expressions occurring in accordance with the universal law of polarity, this being the division of the unified Divine into a masculine and a feminine half, into the Goddess and the God, the Divine and Universal Mother and the Divine and Universal Father. These expressions of the Divine have been known by many different names, the Divine Mother sometimes being known as "the Divine Heart" and the Divine Father being known sometimes as "the Divine Mind". The angelic continuum was born through the *heart* of the Divine from the Divine Mother whereas mankind was made manifest through the Divine Father, through the *mind* of the Divine. The angelic continuum then you see is intimately connected with the Divine Mother, although in various religions that exist upon the planet at this moment in time Angels are looked upon as being solely from the Divine Father, to the patriarchal expression of the Source.

Shekinah is the true face of the Divine Mother presence. The Goddess Sophia, an expression of this Universal Mother, is often viewed as being angelic in nature, a Goddess who is surrounded by many wings in a similar vein to the Elohim, Cherubim or Seraphim. She is considered to be the face of the mother of the Angels, the Goddess from which the angelic beings were born. And in essence this is true, for Angels are the expressions of the Divine's love given form and action, given motion. They are the Divine's fingers and toes, its hands, that that was created in order to set in motion the material universe into which the Divine breathed its light and life. They are love in motion, they are wisdom in action, they are a combination of the Divine Mother's desire to spread her love into the physical universe and the heart of the Divine's active thoughts, the Divine's wisdom, Sophia's wisdom, given form and active existence and life within space and time.

I have always been aligned to the Divine Mother presence. In many of my lifetimes and in the lifetime in which I was Mary I was initially trained in the mysteries of the Divine Mother and later became a teacher of these mysteries, long after these mysteries had been abandoned by the temples that originally taught them. These mysteries had been hand-ed down to my people from generation to generation from the Atlantean survivors who brought to the greater world the true original teachings of the Divine that had been given to them by the angelic beings at the beginning. This alignment to the Divine Mother presence has enabled me at times to be a living avatar for her energy here on Earth, to be a physical conduit through which her energy would shine, aligning and linking me powerfully to the presence and core energy of the angelic continuum. This core energy, as I have said, is love. The Angels are the Divine's love made manifest in reality and everything they have been entrusted to do, everything they have been guided to bring into manifestation and watch over, has been born through love; through the Divine's love for knowledge, for experience, through the Divine's love for its creation, the material universe and the life forms that exist inside it. Love is one of the primary motivating emotions which exists as the underlying force within all of creation.

Ironically, here on Earth, love is also one of the forces which creates the most chaos and disharmony. It is mankind's innate and unquenchable need for love that causes them not only to create beauty and wonder and to express their divinity through science and spirituality alike but also to create war and aggression and conflict and horror and pain. It is mankind's need for love and acceptance from each other and from God that has caused them to feel disconnected from that that they seek. Hungry for that that is all around them. Desperate for that that they are part of. Mankind has always sought favour from their Creator. They have always hungered for the presence and touch of the Divine. But their fall from grace, their sinking in the ever densifying vibration of the material world, has stolen from them the awareness that the Divine is all around them and that they themselves are divine. They have become separated in sense only from the presence of the Universal Mother and Father that exists in nature, that exists in the finer vibratory realms all around them and that exists within their own hearts and being. It has been their rather desperate and clumsy attempts to reconnect with the Divine Presence that has caused them to create religions, modify truths, alter the course of ancient wisdoms, so that they might draw themselves closer to that place, to that presence that they imagine to be God. They have created structures and rules to explain things away, to detail why things are as they are and to stipulate how things can be achieved. They have created, out of a sense of forgetfulness, from illusion, rules and regulations that they believe will make them more holy, more favoured and loved by the Divine, and they have written these into the existing universal truths and laws that were left by the Divine for them as instructions whereby they might live their life and *naturally* draw closer to the realisation of their own divinity.

When different members of their global society have produced different laws and rules, different comprehensions and understandings of the original mystery teachings and truths, they have entered into conflict with them believing that only one race could be right and this conflict, this clash of theological belief has created war and political unrest. It has been the root cause of all of the primary destructive forces that have ever been raised throughout your world. All this for love and acceptance, all this because mankind has sought the love of the Divine that has *always* been with them, all this because mankind has sought acceptance from themselves and from their fellow human beings when it stands before them and exists within them continually. All this because of love. Mankind still in this enlightened age believes that they are not worthy of the love of the Divine or of their fellow man if they in some way, shape or form behave outside of the parameters of society's rules and restrictions, outside of the parameters of religion's laws. They believe that if they are sinful, that if they are unjust, if they are lacking purity, if they are not pious, if they are in any way marred or no longer in alignment with the divine template that has been set before them, that they will be cast out, judged and separated from God.

The Divine Source is non-judgemental. It is unconditional in nature. It cares not what you do but only who you are. It sees the light of your soul buried beneath the illusionary construct of your ego, the armour that has been created around that part of you which is eternal and divine, by society and religion and the political machinations of your history. It does not care if you are not pure of body or of mind, it does not care if you have indulged in practices in the past which have been far from benign. It cares only for that part of you which is eternal and infinite, which is divine, which is truly real and which can transcend your own history and rise to the surface like a flower journeying through the dark soil towards the light.

Mankind uses a tremendous amount of their energy holding the love of the Divine at bay. They create excuses and reasons and they adopt beliefs held by others and they forge an armour, a force field of self-loathing around themselves to hold the abundant, loving presence of God aside when all they need do is relax, is let go, is open themselves to the overwhelming, infinite and eternal presence of the Divine love.

Here then is a small ritual that can be performed to help you release your barriers, to give you pause from the constant creation of the excuses that you forge in order to hold the Divine at bay. It is called "the Ritual of Angelic Welcoming". It is an invitation to let the presence and love of the Divine into your life. It is, as all divine things are, very simple.

RITUAL

Light a candle of any colour and place beside it if you will other things that are evocative of the Divine. A flower, some incense, a cross or other religious symbol, a picture of something that evokes in you a divine response, of nature, of the sun and moon, of a saint or Angel, a picture that depicts the

Divine in some way. However complicated or simple your altar may be is irrelevant. It is personal to you and therefore can be beautiful and elaborate or simple and succinct.

Sit before it and make sure that you will not be disturbed and take some time to relax. Adjust your posture. Make sure that you are comfortable and warm. Make sure that there is no stress or tension in your neck or shoulders, in your face or hands or feet, that your back is well supported. That you are sitting upright and comfortable and relaxed. Take three deep breaths in and as you breathe them out sigh them out loudly, noisily, encouraging yourself to release into these out breaths internal tension, stress, negativity, worry, doubt and concern. And when you have completed these breaths take a few moments to sit in the peace. Try to bring your thoughts focused and present into the moment, giving yourself time to let go of any niggling distractions, and when you feel present in the moment, when you feel grounded, read out these words:

"From the North, from the Earth, from trees deep rooted and mountains high, I call the Angels, come to me, bearing the Divine's love.

From the East, from the Air, from winds and breezes, gales and storms, I call the Angels, come to me, bearing the Divine's love.

From the South, from the Fire, from volcanoes, from hearths and candle flames, I call the Angels, come to me, bearing the Divine's love.

From the West, from the Water, from seas and oceans, rivers and streams, from the rain that falls from heaven, I call the Angels, come to me, bearing the Divine's love.

From Above and from Below, from the centre and the surround, from the spaces in between, from Spirit, I call the Angels, come to me, bearing the Divine's love.

I release my boundaries, I release my shield, I sacrifice my resistance and openly accept the presence of the Angels, the presence of the Divine, of the heart and mind of the universe, of the Mother and the Father of all. I invite you and welcome you come, come to me, bearing love, and fill me with your presence until I overflow."

Sit within the space, feel the presence draw close and near, let it fill you from the tips of your toes to the top of your head until you are submerged in the solution of the Divine love. Until you overflow, until you are washed away in this presence. Sit within this space for a while and be still and then after some time give thanks in your own words to the Divine for this opportunity of communion, to the Universal Father and the Universal Mother, to the Angels who have come. But do not stop there. Give thanks for those things that life has given you: joy, health, happiness, sunshine, birdsong, food, companionship, love, family, history, the future, dreams, for colours and sounds, for music and songs, for the sweet things in life that make life bearable, joyful, good. Through acts of gratitude we tie ourselves to the presence of the Divine. We tie ourselves to the Divine inside ourselves. We strengthen our connection to all that is good.

Once you have done this you can place your armour back upon your body. You can erect the boundary around you if you like, you can shield yourself in your usual way. Inside the armour the love of the Divine Presence will still sing its song and enable you to feel that you belong.

END OF RITUAL

This ritual is a simple one and yet profound. It is powerful because of its simplicity, because it does not work to create something but rather to acknowledge something that exists. It is powerful because it flows in accordance with your own true nature and not against it.

The Divine is all around us, is within us; is everything that is. Try from time to time to remember this and to embrace it. May the love of the Divine Mother and Father eternally shine on your path. With bright blessings I leave you with my love.

◈ SOPHIA ◈

Empowerer of Women

I am Sophia, the Goddess of Wisdom, the bringer of empowerment, the lady of light and love and truth. I am an extension of the consciousness of the Divine, an expression of the Divine Mother's radiance and love. I am an implement of her will, her desire to teach and educate mankind, to empower women and open their consciousness and hearts to the truth. I have always been, since before the beginning of time, within the hearts and minds of men and women. I have been the inspiration and motivation for women to search for truth even when law and culture prohibited them. I have been the desire within the breast of man to seek inside himself the subtle, gentle, loving emotions of the artist and the healer. I am the mother's touch. I am the lover's gaze. I am the gentle caress of light upon the land.

In truth I am no Angel; I am an expression of the Divine but in the past have been seen as Angel and documented as such. Often I am depicted with many wings, holding a chalice of light from which issues forth a flame. Often I am seen as veiled, mysterious, silent and sometimes eternally pregnant with the possibilities of infinite potential and hope. My veil is the veil of mystery that shrouds all those things unseen, secrets hidden by truth. My silence is the silence of those who know the wisdom of using the absence of sound as a mirror to reflect the greater truth which lies always and only within. The flame that issues forth from my chalice is the light of enlightenment which is borne not from the mind, not from academia and intellect but from experience and love. And my wings are the wings that bear us to heaven when we seek not for ourselves but for all of mankind the truth that lies beyond the light of the Divine.

In certain tomes, historical, cultural and religious texts, I am depicted as being the mother of Angels and there is in essence *some* truth in this for it is from the Goddess, the Divine Mother, that angelic life was born. In the highest realms the divine feminine current is seen as the heart of the Source of All, whereas the masculine current is seen as the mind. Angelic beings have all been born from the *heart* of the Divine Source and therefore from the Goddess, where-as mankind was delivered through the *mind* of the Divine, through the God force and its current and energy. As I am an expression of the Divine Mother presence, it would then be true to say that I am mother of all Angels, even though I am not an Angel myself. But it is more important that I bring forward a message today concerning the nature of Angels as perceived through the *feminine* eye, rather than through the patriarchal, Christian perspective, as is more commonly known and understood on Earth.

As you know, Angels are neither male nor female but in truth they are androgynous, a perfect balance of masculine and feminine energy. Their appearance to those who have true sight then is one of an androgynous human, masculine and feminine in countenance combined together. Not hermaphroditic but more aesthetically mysterious. The strength and athletic poise of the man but the grace and gentle demeanour of the woman, the beautiful slender curves of the feminine combined with the masculine power and strength of the male creating a beautiful androgyny, a future vision of mankind's prophesied perfection and an echo or memory of mankind's origin in the ancient days of Lemuria.

Of course, the clairvoyant eye is subject to the consciousness of the individual who uses it and to their cultural and historical conditionings. Those who have been reared to imagine Angels to be men will see them as such. Those who have been indoctrinated into the patriarchal Christian religion will see them in their traditional forms and very rarely, if ever at all, encounter a female Angel or even a female looking Angel. Those with wider perspectives or who have reconditioned themselves to comprehend the universe in a more expansive manner may see Angels as they truly are or indeed may reinterpret the energies that they experience and see them as purely female in nature. Some may call forth the Angels in feminine guise, drawing upon specifically the feminine current of their expression and therefore invoking them in a slightly imbalanced way in order to interact with them in this predominantly female polarity. Of course, the greater truth is that the true bodies of Angels are a combination of harmonic frequencies that manifest through ever interchanging patterns of sacred geometric light and holographic energy. Some have begun to see Angels in this true state though for many it is too impersonal.

I then have come to talk about the value of acknowledging the feminine quality contained within the angelic continuum and the importance of sometimes calling forth angelic energy in imbalanced states in order to access the predominant masculine or feminine polarity of the angelic current. The Angels that exist within the continuum exist in order to represent and embody specific frequencies of universal light and energy. They represent the myriad of vibrations and colours that become divided as the one true light of the Divine enters into the prism of limited space and time.

These rays, these currents of energies, are each specific to a particular desire or need, to a particular speciality, to a particular place or state of consciousness and mind such as earth and air, fire, water, spirit, love, enlightenment, contemplation, karma, alchemy, solitude, sanctuary, silence, peace, hope, healing, joy, introspection, wonder, miracle. Some of these expressions of the divine energy and consciousness are masculine in their polarity and orientation while some are predominantly feminine.

The Angels who represent these feminine energies will therefore have a greater feminine frequency and a greater feminine countenance and some may be seen as being purely feminine in nature: the Angels of love, the Angels of sensuality, of inspiration, of gentleness. All these Angels are predominantly feminine in their current and nature, in the energy that they represent and express and although they in essence are perfectly balanced, the way in which they embody and express this energy at times causes them to focus their energy more in a predominantly feminine form in order to contain and convey this power accurately on Earth. Female Angels then exist in this sense and can be seen and experienced but it is also important to understand that sometimes, even within a balanced element, we will need to call upon it in a masculine or feminine way in order to maximise its efficiency and its use in a particular form here on Earth.

Let us take then fire as an example. The element of fire represents a variety of things. It represents the power of the warrior. It represents passion. It represents transformation. It represents enlightenment. It represents spirit. The power of the warrior is predominantly masculine, it is a dynamic energy, whereas the power of passion and sensuality is predominantly feminine as it is a receptive art. Transformation and alchemy is masculine in its dynamic practice whereas enlightenment is feminine in its truest form because it evokes truth from within. Spirit is a balanced presence, neither masculine nor feminine in predominance but both combined. Therefore when we call upon the energy of fire through the Angels and their angelic chief, the Archangel Michael, we can call upon this Angel in a masculine or feminine guise depending upon the way in which we might use the qualities of this power. It would be more appropriate to call forward the Archangel Michael as a feminine force if we were invoking this power in order to instruct us in the arts of passion and sensuality, or indeed, in order to invoke enlightenment but much more appropriate to call upon Michael as male if we were calling upon this Angel as warrior or protector, or indeed, as alchemist and magician. If we called upon fire as a spiritual force then far better for us to envision this Angel as androgynous, a perfect balance of both.

In the past, certain humans who have worked with angelic forces have seen fit to divide the Angels into both masculine and feminine forms, the feminine counterpart of the Archangel Michael, some say, being the Lady Faith. It is not particularly necessary to divide the Angels in this way, to name the masculine and feminine forms differently, but if the human mind feels more comfortable with this definite division then that is also fine. It is, however, still quite appropriate to work with the Archangel Michael as both male and female. Even though the name is a masculine one it can be applied to the feminine expression of Michael's energy too.

Working with polarity and division is a way of taking responsibility in regards to your knowledge and your application of knowledge in order to bring about result. Hoping that the Divine will provide you with an expression of energy appropriately gendered in order to suit your cause is not presumptuous but it is rather lacking responsibility in regards to the knowledge that you possess and the power that you apply. Far better to use your understanding and more dynamically interact with the mechanics of your universe than sit idly by hoping and praying that the Divine will do everything that you require for you. Growth occurs through conscious interaction with the Divine, not only and always through surrender. Sometimes surrender is nothing more than giving our power away. Therefore we must be cautious of such acts, even when done with the best of intention and in prayer.

Now in regards to my own energy, the energy of empowerment, *feminine* empowerment and the inspiration of wisdom and truth, there are Angels specifically connected to my light and force and being who can be invoked in order to bring the nature of my power to Earth in order to inspire feminine empowerment, in order to awaken the light of truth, in order to encourage from within recognition of the presence of the divine feminine, the Divine Mother, in all life. These are the Angels of Sophia. They emerge on the softest of pink rays. A pink ray which is filled with white light and gently suffused with the palest yellow, like the colours that are seen in the sky when the sun first rises in the morning or sets at night, the most delicate shade of white pink yellow. This is the light of my Angels.

The Angels of Sophia can be very beneficial in preparing a space so that I may enter it, for they are my heralds and harbingers and as such are responsible for rearranging the dynamic energies within locations so that my power and my presence can be more greatly felt and have greater effect. My power is not for women only, though can be powerfully employed in any female endeavour of education or better-ment, empowerment and growth, from the most mundane to the most spiritual and divine. But also my energies can be invoked in order to awaken in men the feminine side of their own psyche; gentleness, love, creativity, inspiration, nurturing and self-nurturing, sensuality, sensitivity and passion.

Here then is a small ritual to call upon the Angels of Sophia to aid and assist you in any of these purposes that I have mentioned.

RITUAL

In the space in which you wish the Angels of Sophia to work their magick, still the room around you. Light incense, frankincense, rose, jasmine or lemongrass and play music of a soft, melodious and gentle kind. Light a single candle, pale pink, white or pale yellow, prepared on a small altar, deco-rated maybe with a cloth of white or pink or pale yellow, adorned with a few crystals connected to the energy of my ray; rose quartz, pearl, selenite, gypsum, coral. And here, once you have silenced and stilled yourself, speak this prayer:

"Great Sophia, expression of the Divine Mother of all, empowerer of women, Goddess of wisdom and light, hear my prayer. Send into this space the Angels of your brilliance and heart that they may prepare this space for the coming of your energy and light that they may cast away all doubt, all darkness and all fear, opening this space to learning, truth and peace, to sensuality, love and grace, to honour and understanding in truth. Let this space be a space in which your brilliant and dazzling heart and mind may enter and inspire all those within it with your wonder, beauty and grace, opening them to the divine feminine within all."

Envision before you in the air, level with your own heart, a chalice forming a brilliant pale yellow light. The chalice is filled with a sparkling, inner, white luminescence that begins to erupt from it as a holy fire. The fire twists and turns and rises into a tornado of flame, a tornado of flame which is the hosts of Sophia, the Angels of Sophia's light. From this tornado of flame they spin out into the room, transforming and clearing the energy, lightening the vibration, kissing the space with light until it brims with radiance and brilliance, until the whole space is filled with luminescent wonder. At this point they pause to hold the energy in place and then return to the spinning tornado of flame, which descends slowly into the chalice, which slowly dissipates into the wondrous light of the room.

The room will be held in this space, a welcoming space, into which my presence may be invoked or simply into which your intention may be placed in regards to the nature of the energy, my energy, that you wish to invoke here for at least a day, longer if you place greater intent and statement behind your initial invocation. Continual invocation of this energy will lead to a dedication of this space to my presence and the power will begin to grow and be sustainable for lengthier and lengthier periods of time.

END OF RITUAL

Now is the time for mankind and womankind to grow in power and recognise that the Divine is not predominantly masculine but also feminine in nature. Now is the time for man and womankind to open their hearts and release the feminine light of their psyche. To draw closer to becoming what they once were: a perfect androgyny of male and female, co-joined in a sacred harmony and marriage of balance.

My power can aid you in achieving this; my power can aid you in finding your strength as woman or man through the feminine, through the Divine Mother. My power is the harbinger of the return of the Magdalene Flame, the feminine Christ. My power is part of the way and is not to be ignored any longer.

Take then these final words as blessing as you go upon your way. May the gentle light of dawn's breaking fall upon you and bless you with its rays. May it warm your weary and cold bones and kiss your skin with love. May your mind be open to truth and your heart to the new experiences of life, may your feet be guided by wisdom to the right people and places and your thoughts inspired with continuous questioning for truth. Know that I am with you, the mother of all creation, the bringer of wisdom and light, the love of divinity, of understanding, and let me quest by your side and guide you as you search for the eternal truths that will lead you home. In perfect love and perfect trust may this be so. So mote it be. Amen.

ETZIEKAEL

✦ Epilogue ✦

This book is alive. It is alive with our presence and our light and our love. It is filled with our consciousness and our truth and our teaching and it is a gift extended from our realm to you. Since the beginning of time, Angels have been in existence with one primary function and one primary function only: to guide mankind towards their ultimate point of evolution, to guide mankind towards unity with the Divine. This guidance takes many different shapes and forms; teaching and healing, rituals and ceremonies of initiation and communion, guiding presences that steer each and every person upon the planet towards the fulfilment of their individual destiny and life purpose.

It does not matter whether you are an intellectual or someone who prefers a simpler comprehension of truth and life. It does not matter if you do not understand some of the more complicated philosophies outlined by some of those Angels who have spoken their truth and teaching in this book. It does not matter if you only ever call upon our presence for simple blessings, guidance and truth. It matters only that you acknowledge that we are here, that we are universal spiritual presences, that we are an extension of the Divine Consciousness and that we can be called upon and drawn upon to aid and assist you with your spiritual growth.

For some, the information contained within this book will

be challenging. It will test them, encouraging them to see themselves and their world from a perspective that they are not used to. It will challenge their perspective of Angels and they may find some of the information here unpalatable and not true. Each and every person must take responsibility for their own beliefs, they must use their discernment when reading or hearing truth outlined to them by someone who claims to have received it from a higher spiritual source and decide themselves whether or not they will make that truth their own. This book is not about conversion. It is not about taking away your perception of your world and replacing it with our own. It is a sharing, an opportunity for you to indulge yourself in a different perspective so as to encourage you to contemplate another potential truth and see how this might fit with the understanding that you already possess regarding the world in which you live.

Words are powerful, whether written or spoken. They affect us in ways that we often do not comprehend, touching the deeper and more unconscious parts of our awareness. Each and every human being has the capacity inside them to recognise truth. It is part of their divine inheritance and as such, if you read these words with an open heart you will feel the presence of the Divine within them and you will know which words for you at this moment in time are true, which words you must hear and act upon.

This book is for sharing. It is to be passed on and read aloud. It is to be offered to others, worked with in groups. It is something which will in time hopefully inspire change and transformation in many. It is a companion. Something that you can keep with you, that can travel the path by your side and aid and assist you when you feel alone and confused, when you feel surrounded by darkness and devoid of the presence of the Divine. It is a lifeline. It is a guiding star. It is magickal north on your soul's compass, something to turn to when there is no one else. It is a reminder that whispers simply and sweetly in your ear "you are not alone".

The greatest gifts are given in love. They are not valued because of their material worth. They are not valued because they are sought after by others. They are valued because of the love which is contained within their structure. Whether this book has been bought for you by another or by yourself or has come into your possession by some strange coincidence or quirk of nature, by some synchronicity, whether you have borrowed it from a library or found it in the street, it has been given to you by the Angels as a gift of their love. It has come to you now because it is the right time for you to hear the words within these pages, for you to work with the concepts and truths that are offered to you by the Angels. Whether you see it immediately or whether the realisation dawns upon you slowly at some point in the future, it is important for you to recognise and know that this book is our hand openly extended to you in love. It is given as a gift of light and truth. Openheartedly then read the pages. Thumb through the rituals and ceremonies. Read aloud the prayers and as you do, open yourself to the presence of the Divine's love as it enters into your room, into your home, into your heart, and know that we are near.

I am Etziekael, the Angelic Scribe; the presence that has enabled this book to be written. Mine are the last words within it and they speak a blessing upon it and upon all those who read of its pages.

"May the light of love and truth, may the power of passion and inspiration, may the gift of the Divine, bless and be with you always. May you be surrounded and showered in light, held in love, blessed by truth and guided always by your true heart's desire. In perfect love and perfect trust, bright blessed be."

ABOUT THE AUTHOR

Edwin Courtenay is a clairvoyant, channel and non-traditional solitary practitioner of Wicca. He has been communing with the world of Spirit since he was 4 years old and actively began developing his gifts aged 16. He teaches, lectures and provides consultations from the College of Psychic Studies in London as well as working throughout the U.K. and overseas. He is author of two other books, *The Ascended Masters' Book of Ritual and Prayer* and *Reflections – The Masters Remember* and has produced a guided meditation CD called *Angel Kiss* with Rachael Kelly on how to connect with your Guardian Angel. Edwin lives in Newcastle in the UK with his partner Andrew. For up-to-date information on Edwin's diary of events plus his latest messages from the spirit world go to his website at www.edwincourtenay.co.uk or email him at:

bluestarofwonder@hotmail.com

BY THE SAME AUTHOR

Many people are fascinated by the idea of reincarnation, yet it is important to live fully in the here and now. So it is not this book's intention to promote an escape from reality but rather to show how memories from past lives can actually help us to walk the path of our current life.

For this reason the Masters have decided to speak about who they were in past lives and what they have learnt. Saint Germain tells us about his lives as Merlin, Christopher Columbus, Francis Bacon and Saint Germain; Jesus speaks of his time in Atlantis and Serapis Bey of his experiences as an incarnate angel. Also read the stories of Lady Portia, Kwan Yin, Mother Mary, Mary Magdalene and Djwal Khul.

The themes of their lives are mirrored in our lives: the search for our own identity, our relationships, finding our life purpose, self acceptance, surrender and compassion.

Be comforted, embraced and enchanted
by the stories in this book.

168 pages, paperback, 13 x 20,9 cm, ISBN 978-3-929345-20-9

The Prince of the Stars

BY THE SAME AUTHOR

Most of us would like to change in some way but don't know what to do about it. This book contains very practical rituals that we can carry out, focusing the power of our inner divinity to set in motion the changes we would like to see.

Thirteen Ascended Masters (among them Saint Germain, Mother Mary, Jesus and Kwan Yin) provide us with simple rituals to improve various aspects of our lives. These rituals will also strengthen our connection with the Source and awaken our dormant powers. The Ascended Masters reach out their hands full of love and want to give us a glimpse of the splendor of the Divine. This book helps us to find the way back.

„A remarkable little gem of a book. Every word is measured and contributes to a seamless, elegant conception with passages of serene and universal application. An extraordinary distillation of spiritual teaching."

Colourama Magazine

128 pages, paperback, 13 x 20,9 cm, ISBN 978-3-929345-08-7

The Prince of the Stars